# FRENCHIE

# FRENCHIE

## New Bistro Cooking

## Greg **Marchand**

Principal photography by **Djamel Dine Zitout**

ARTISAN
New York

Published by Artisan
A division of Workman Publishing Company, Inc.
225 Varick Street
New York, NY 10014-4381
artisanbooks.com

Published simultaneously in Canada by Thomas Allen & Son, Limited

......................................................................................................................................................

Library of Congress Cataloging-in-Publication Data
Marchand, Greg.
  [Cuisine du Frenchie at Home. English]
  Frenchie / Greg Marchand ; photographs by Djamel Dine Zitout. — First American edition.
      pages cm
  Translation of: La Cuisine du Frenchie at Home.
  Includes index.
  ISBN 978-1-57965-534-1
  1. Cooking, French. 2. Restaurant Frenchie (Paris, France) I. Title.
  TX719.M3128 2014
  641.5944—dc23

                                                                    2013029979

......................................................................................................................................................

Published by arrangement with Éditions Alternatives, which originally published this book
in France under the title *La Cuisine du Frenchie at Home.*

Translation by Camille Labro
Printed in China
First American edition, March 2014

10 9 8 7 6 5 4 3 2 1

To my children, Tom and Lily

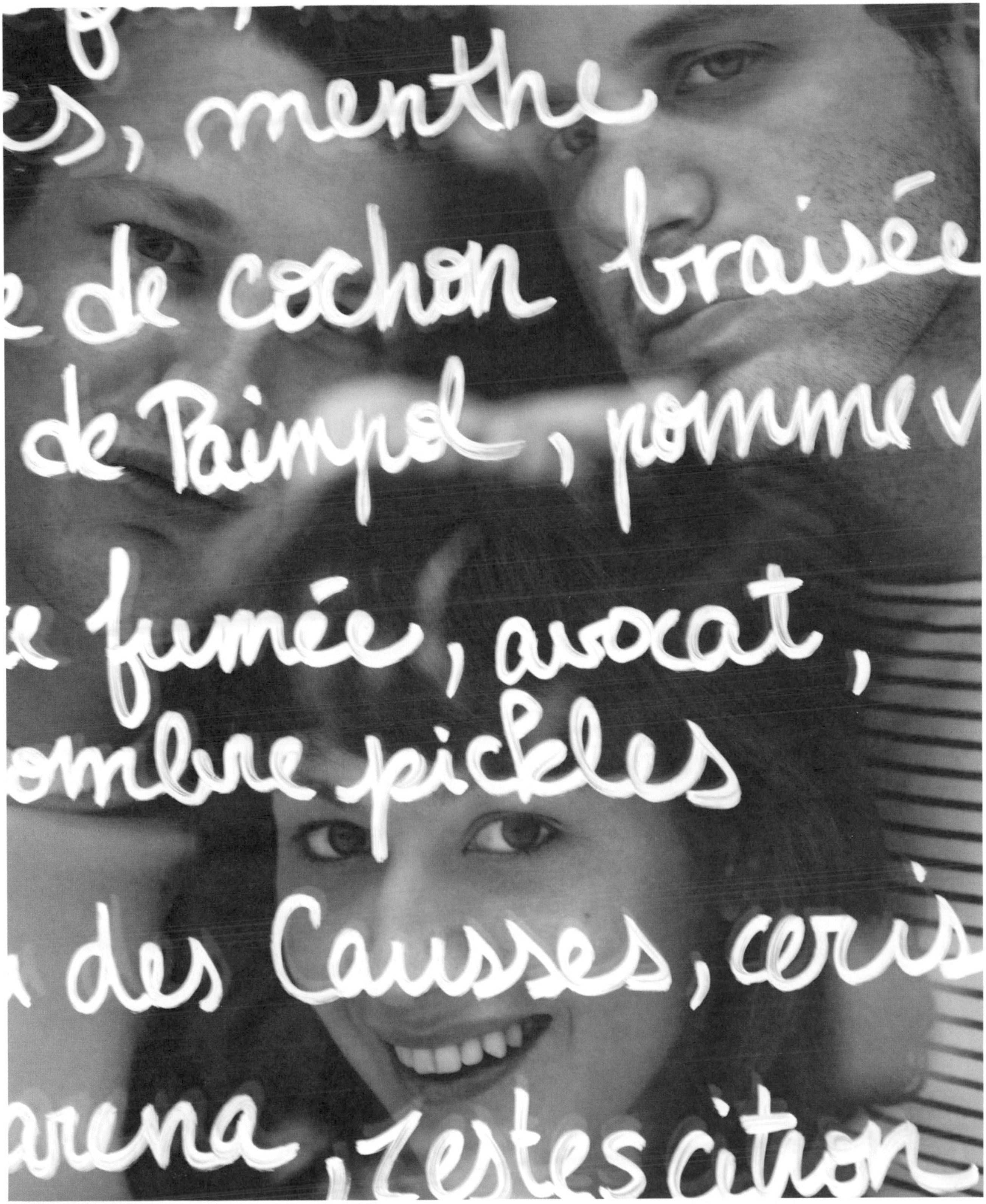

s, menthe
e de cochon braisée
de Paimpol, pomme v
e fumée, avocat,
ombre pickles
des Causses, ceris
arena, zestes citron

# Contents

# Introduction

When I worked at Jamie Oliver's restaurant Fifteen on Old Street in London, he nicknamed me "Frenchie" because I was the only French person in the kitchen. The nickname stuck (new members of the staff never even learned my real name), and that's how it came to pass that my restaurant in Paris is called Frenchie.

At Fifteen, every year we'd hire fifteen kids from disadvantaged backgrounds and train them in the kitchen. I identified with these young apprentices, having had my own share of troubled times. I'd started to cook when I was fifteen, in the orphanage where I grew up, in Nantes.

The chef was off on weekends, and I was more than happy to volunteer to cook: it gave me a break from the craziness of the orphanage courtyard. The first dish I ever made was *escalope normande*, veal with mushrooms and cream. Although it was probably poorly executed, the joy it generated in the other kids was enough to persuade me to enroll in cooking school. To this day, pleasing people, seeing the smiles on their faces when they take their first bite of a dish I have made, fills me with pleasure.

I entered cooking school in Brittany at sixteen, sporting long hair, a skull ring, and a Metallica patch on my jean jacket—I thought I looked so cool! But the teachers didn't agree. I was quickly dispatched to the barber and then to buy a couple of cheap suits, some black socks, and a pair of black shoes. My love affair with hard rock went the way of the long hair.

I had a lot to sort out in my life back then. That I got through my studies was nothing short of a miracle, but I did graduate, having learned the basics of French cuisine, restaurant health and sanitation rules, and the ins and outs of the hospitality business. With good luck, I soon landed a job in London with David Nicholls at the Mandarin Oriental in Knightsbridge. It was my first experience working as part of a large brigade with very high standards. I realize now that my passion for cooking was born then and there: it was the first time in my life that I felt part of something—a clan, a posse, a family, all centered on cooking. I was happy to get up and go to work, and I learned something new every day. That was my best cooking school ever. And I loved the energy of London, the curries served on Brick Lane and the full English breakfast at the greasy spoon where we would go on our days off, after a night of drinking.

When the restaurant closed for renovation, I got myself transferred to the Mandarin Oriental in Hong Kong, where I worked at Jean-Georges Vongerichten's Vong. The menu was a perfect fusion of French and Asian cooking, foie gras and mango, duck and tamarind, and all kinds of crazy things I had never seen before. I had a blast in Hong Kong, but I had to return to London to be part of the reopening team there. We had a brand-new kitchen with a wok, a tandoori oven, and a wood-fired oven. It was awesome: I was cooking new dishes and discovering new ingredients every day. But I didn't get on very well with the new head chef. One day he verbally abused me so badly that I packed up my knives, handed him my apron, and left.

Years of London weather had left me yearning for the sun, so I flew off to Andalusia and worked on the beach in a *chiringuito* (beach bar), making fresh fish *a la plancha*, octopus *a la gallega*, tortillas, and all sorts of tapas. Cooking barefoot in the sand felt good, but I needed more of a challenge. That test came in the person of Arthur Potts Dawson, previously a sous chef at The River Café in London, who was opening a restaurant in Marbella. I became his sous chef, and the food we did there was inspired by The Café: simple regional Italian cuisine made with great fresh ingredients. It was my first real exposure to Italian cooking. We even had a wood-burning oven and turned out great pizza. What a year!

Then Arthur was offered a good position in London, where I followed him. That's when I landed at Fifteen, where I eventually became head chef. It's difficult enough to run a restaurant with a team of dedicated chefs—imagine having a team of kids struggling with the simple idea of having to work every day! But we did very well, and when I see that most of them are now professional chefs, spread out around the world, it makes me proud. I also learned respect for ingredients from Jamie's "less is more" approach, and I learned how to keep a business afloat and manage a staff—all with the thought of opening my own place one day. But I wasn't ready, and New York beckoned.

Once I arrived in New York City, I tried out at a few restaurants, and when Michael Anthony, the newly appointed chef at Gramercy Tavern, offered me a job, I jumped at the chance to work there. My girlfriend (and soon-to-be wife), Marie, and I found a nice little apartment in Greenpoint, a Polish neighborhood in Brooklyn. When I came out of the subway, I felt as if I were in Warsaw, with everybody speaking Polish and delis selling Polish charcuterie and other specialties. I immersed myself in New York's rich melting-pot culture. Japan, Korea, Italy, and Mexico, to name a few, were all less than a forty-minute subway ride away, and it was a great inspiration to have products from all over the world so readily available.

On my days off, Marie and I would try different restaurants, from three-stars to little Chinese joints, from newly opened places to established older restaurants. Traveling farther afield, we ate our way through Chicago, San Francisco and the Napa Valley, Florida, and upstate New York. All these experiences gave me more and more ideas about what my own place could be like. Everywhere I went, I took notes in my little Moleskine book about what I found great in each place, from menu holders to the lighting to food, of course, as well as the organization of the dining rooms and menus.

My time in Spain was an advantage in the Gramercy Tavern kitchen. Although my

Spanish was basic, I knew enough to be able to carry on a conversation with the many Hispanic staff members, which made my work easier. Working at the Tavern was a transformative experience. My food is still inspired by Michael's farm-to-table style, and my sense of hospitality is totally informed by the genius of Danny Meyer.

After a year, however, Marie learned she was pregnant. I was very excited about being a dad, but it happened much faster than we'd planned. And we didn't have good health insurance, my visa was going to expire, and Marie had had trouble finding a suitable job. Yet I also felt ready: it was time to go home, after more than ten years on the road. I sadly handed in my notice, and we packed our stuff and flew back to Paris.

When we arrived there, in September 2008, we were jobless and almost penniless. We rented a tiny apartment in Montmartre and I applied for unemployment. I knew I had very little time to launch my project, as cash was running out and Marie was due in December. After exploring several different neighborhoods, I found a spot I really liked on an improbable, deserted cobblestoned street called rue du Nil, tucked away in the garment district. My friends thought I was crazy, but I loved the location. We were a few steps from the busy rue Montorgueil and Les Halles, the historic area known as "the belly of Paris," home until 1971 of the great wholesale marketplace through which all the foods served in Parisian restaurants passed. It made perfect sense.

Yet it was 2008, and the economic crisis was at its worst: I couldn't persuade any bankers to go along with my project, so I got a loan from a friend who, perhaps ironically, was an investment broker. Within two short weeks, we'd scraped the ugly paint from the walls, replaced the bar, and brought in some secondhand furniture. On April Fool's Day 2009, Frenchie opened.

I really had no idea what was happening on the Paris scene, what was hot and what was not: all I wanted to do was to create a place that was the sum of all my best experiences. I wanted to serve simple yet inventive food, using high-quality ingredients, in a laid-back bistro setting, with affordable prices, a menu that changed daily, and a short but exciting wine list. I guess I was in the right place at the right time: the Paris "bistronomy" trend was just starting, and the type of food and ambience I had in mind seemed to be exactly what people were craving. Frenchie quickly received great praise from the public as well as the critics. The phone started to ring nonstop, and the reservation book was filled a month ahead. To this day, I still don't understand how it all happened so quickly.

Two years after opening Frenchie, I took over the lease of a minuscule shop across the street and turned it, after another few months of intense renovations, into Frenchie Bar à Vins. The idea was to offer small plates to go along with great wines on a first-come, first-served basis. The only equipment we had was a fridge, a small grill, and a blowtorch. We designed a clever little menu with that in mind: braised pig's head, hot-smoked trout, seasonal salads, homemade terrines, charcuterie, cheese, and grandma-style tarts. It was an instant hit.

When the shop next door to the bar freed up, we were able to extend the space, which meant more hard construction work. We launched the Wine Bar V2 in July 2012.

At the same time, two of my favorite produce suppliers, Samuel Nahon and Alexandre Drouard of Terroirs d'Avenir, were looking for a space out of which to sell their fantastic fruits and vegetables, fish, and meat to the public (they had been supplying only chefs). I told them about a space two doors away from the restaurant, and soon enough, Terroirs d'Avenir opened a fruit and vegetable store, as well as a butcher shop and a fish market, all on my little street. If you can't go to your suppliers, make them come to you, I say. Imagine being able to go to work every morning and create your menu with what looks best on the shelves that day. No more worries about running out of something when most of the ingredients I use are available right next door!

In the middle of all that, I was offered a book contract. I was super-busy and almost declined the offer, but so many customers had asked me how I did this and

how I cooked that. What a great opportunity to fulfill my guests' requests! So, after careful consideration and planning, I agreed to do a book for the home cook. I would take recipes from the restaurant and strip them down to the essentials. After *La Cuisine du Frenchie at Home* was published, in 2012, the opportunity to do an English version arose; I didn't hesitate for a second.

As I write these lines, the latest kid on the block, Frenchie to Go, has just opened its doors. It's my version of a take-out counter, inspired by my time in New York and London, with everything homemade, from pastrami to hot dogs, maple-syrup bacon to pulled pork, ginger beer to even doughnuts—all made with carefully selected ingredients and rare-breed animals. It's a fun, lively place, where one can come for great coffee and great food all day long, the type of joint where, when I lived abroad, I loved to hang out on my days off. Rue du Nil is now buzzing with all sorts of great food, and we are dedicated to making the best of it. So please, if you are in Paris, come and visit us.

I hope you will enjoy these simple but inventive dishes. They are full of the flavors I came to love in the culinary encounters I had cooking around the world. But I didn't write this book to show you what I could do: I wanted to show you what *you* can do.

## about the recipes

Happily, you'll find lots of dishes in these pages that come together very quickly, such as the Roasted Carrot, Orange, and Avocado Salad (page 28) or the Spanish Ham, Corn, Bell Peppers, and Kaffir Lime (page 78). Others have long cooking times, like the Pork Braised in Milk with Marinated Fennel (page 94), but I think you'll agree that the time is well spent.

In all the recipes, I strive for the excitement you get from contrast, whether it's the smokiness and acidity of the smoked trout on page 58, the bitterness and sweetness of the bitter greens salad on page 108, or the creaminess and crunchiness of the risotto on page 86. Throughout, you may note my fondness for a zing of citrus, for pickles (whether radish, ginger, mustard seed, or other), for the earthiness of mushrooms and nuts, and for the chutneys I fell in love with when I was working in England.

Although the recipes are divided by season and are loosely arranged from starters to desserts, any of the savory dishes could easily serve as a meal. In my cooking, the distinction between starter and main course is more about portion size than anything else—just double the recipe and a salad becomes a meal. Cheese is traditionally served before dessert or as a dessert, especially when married to sweet flavors, such as the Blue Cheese, Lemon Zest and Amarena Cherries (page 42). But I also like to serve it as a salad appetizer or a stand-alone dish, especially the Fresh Peaches, Smoked Mozzarella, and Aged Balsamic (page 70) or the Pear, Turnip, and Pecorino Pepato Salad (page 102). While many people imagine the French still eat three-course meals every day, we tend more and more to appreciate a single course or little plates to share, such as those served at Wine Bar.

At Frenchie, we are very attached to the wines we serve. We work closely with our winemakers, and our sommeliers, Laura and Aurélien, have paired each recipe in this book with a specific wine that we offer at the restaurant. For most of these choices, we have indicated the type of grape and the name of the winemaker. We've also provided a list of wine merchants who may sell these wonderful wines in your part of the world (see Sources, page 137).

Lastly, you may note that we rounded off measurements for ingredients, so volume and ounce measures don't always correspond exactly to the metric measurements provided. The recipes will work fine no matter which measurements you use, but I encourage you to buy a digital scale and try your hand at cooking metric—it's so much easier.

Now off to the kitchen to get your hands dirty!

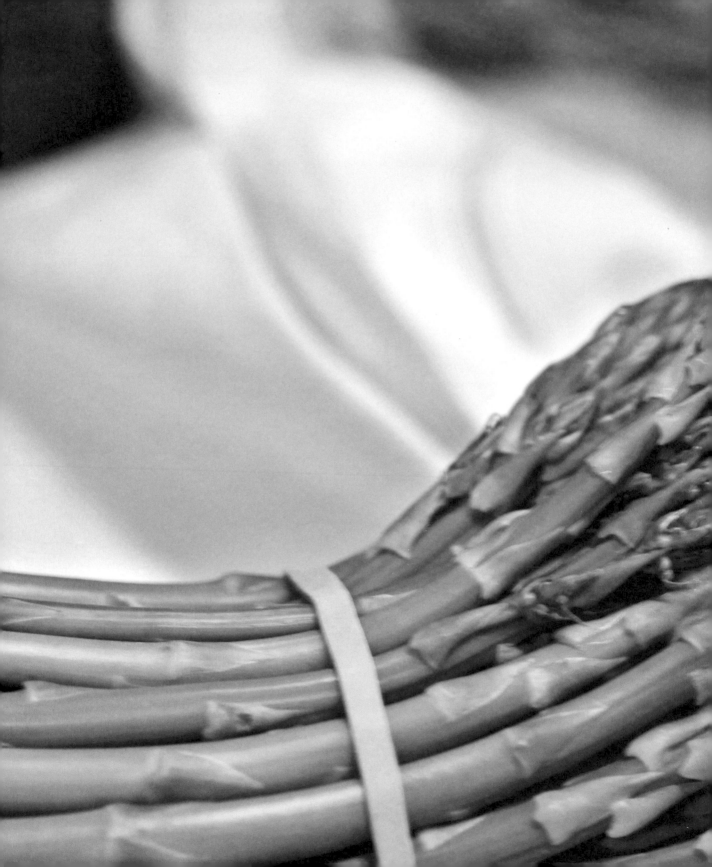

# spring

# Foie Gras
## with Cherry Chutney

**6 to 8 servings / Wine pairing: Vouvray demi-sec (Chenin Blanc); Vincent Carême**

This technique for making *foie gras au torchon* (foie gras cooked in a dish towel) allows you to easily achieve this high-end restaurant dish at home. Letting the foie gras age at least three days is very important, as it only gets better over time.

**EQUIPMENT**
An instant-read thermometer
Kitchen string

**FOR THE FOIE GRAS**
1 vacuum-packed Grade A foie gras
   (about 1 pound/454 grams),
   preferably already deveined
Fleur de sel
Crushed black pepper

**FOR THE CHERRY CHUTNEY**
1 small onion
2 shallots
1 garlic clove
2½ pounds (1.2 kg.) Bing cherries
5½ tablespoons red wine vinegar
3 tablespoons sugar
2 tablespoons grated fresh ginger
Salt

1 tablespoon chopped chives
Red wine vinegar
Extra virgin olive oil
Fleur de sel
Crushed black pepper
12 to 16 brandied cherries
A handful of baby greens
Juice of ½ lemon, or to taste

## The foie gras

Fill a large pot with water and bring it to 160°F. Add the foie gras, in its sous-vide bag, and cook for 20 minutes, checking the thermometer to make sure the temperature stays at 160°F. Transfer the foie gras to a plate and let cool to room temperature.

Remove the foie gras from the bag and, if necessary, carefully remove the veins with a small knife. Season with fleur de sel and crushed pepper.

Place the foie gras on three 20-inch-long sheets of plastic wrap stacked on top of each other. Pressing and rolling, form the foie gras into a 2-inch-thick log. Tie the ends with kitchen string: the log should be very tight and firm. With a toothpick, poke the wrap all over to remove any air bubbles. Roll up the log in another sheet of plastic wrap and tie it tightly with string. Refrigerate for at least 3 days or, ideally, for 1 week.

## The cherry chutney

Meanwhile, peel and finely chop the onion, shallots, and garlic. Pit the cherries.

Bring the vinegar and sugar to a boil in a pot over medium-high heat, stirring to dissolve the sugar. Add the onion, shallots, garlic, and ginger. Season with ¼ teaspoon salt and cook over low heat for about 2 minutes, just until slightly softened. Add the cherries and simmer gently, mashing the cherries a bit with the back of a wooden spoon to help release their juices, for 10 minutes, or until the mixture is the consistency of a chunky chutney. Taste and add salt if necessary. Transfer to a jar and let cool. (The chutney can be refrigerated for several months; it makes a great condiment for cheese.)

## Finishing touches

Put 6 tablespoons of the chutney in a small bowl and stir in the chives, a dash of red wine vinegar, and a drizzle of olive oil. Season with fleur de sel.

Dip the blade of a sharp knife into very hot water, wipe it dry, and cut the foie gras into 1-inch-thick slices, reheating the knife as necessary. Remove the plastic wrap from each slice and glisten each one with a drop of olive oil. Season with a pinch each of fleur de sel and crushed pepper.

Place a slice of foie gras, a spoonful of chutney, and 2 cherries on each plate. Lightly season the baby greens with olive oil, lemon juice, and fleur de sel and arrange on the plates.

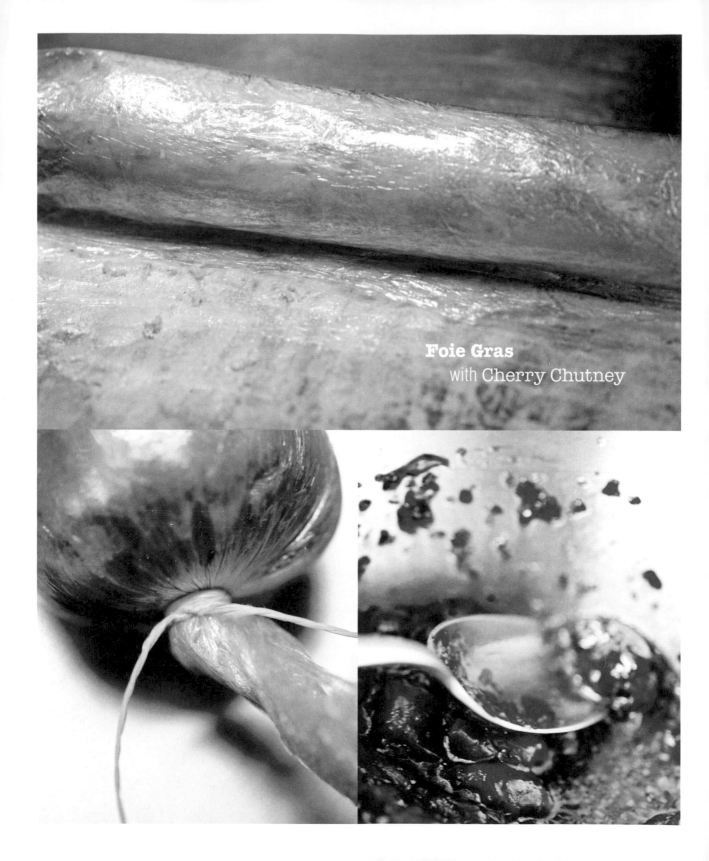

**Foie Gras** with Cherry Chutney

# Roasted Carrot, *Orange,* and **Avocado Salad**

4 servings / Wine pairing: Touraine white (Sauvignon Blanc); Jean-François Mérieau

This is a dish I could eat every day. Simple, quick, and delicious, it combines the crunchiness and sweetness of carrots, the zing of orange, and the meaty texture of avocado.

**FOR THE ROASTED CARROTS**
2 bunches (about 1 pound/454 grams) baby carrots
¼ teaspoon coriander seeds
¼ teaspoon fennel seeds
1 thyme sprig

1 garlic clove, crushed
Olive oil
Salt

**FOR THE SALAD**
2 to 3 navel oranges

2 avocados
3 cilantro sprigs
Juice of 1 lime, or to taste
Olive oil
Fleur de sel
Piment d'Espelette

## The roasted carrots

Preheat the oven to 350°F.

Trim the carrots and put them in a bowl.

Toast the coriander and fennel seeds in a small dry skillet over medium heat until fragrant, about 3 minutes; take care not to burn them. Let cool, then coarsely crush the seeds with a mortar and pestle or under a heavy skillet.

Add the toasted spices to the carrots, along with the thyme, garlic, a drizzle of olive oil, and a pinch of salt, and toss well with your hands. Transfer the carrots to a baking dish and roast for 20 to 25 minutes, until tender and lightly browned. Set aside.

## The salad

With a sharp knife, peel the oranges down to the flesh, removing all the bitter white pith, then slice into ¼-inch-thick rounds; you need 16 slices. Cut the avocados in half, remove the pits, peel, and cut lengthwise into thick slices. Remove the cilantro leaves from the stems.

## To serve

Combine the carrots, oranges, and avocados in a medium bowl. Sprinkle with the cilantro, lime juice, olive oil, fleur de sel, and a pinch of piment d'Espelette and toss gently. Arrange on salad plates and serve.

*Roasted Carrot*, Orange, and **Avocado Salad**

# Wild **Garlic Broth** with *Fresh Crabmeat*

4 servings / Wine pairing: Savoie white (Altesse); Adrien Berlioz

This starter combines the subtle bitterness of fragrant citrons with the sweetness of crabmeat and the delicacy of blanched wild garlic leaves. Wild garlic is a broad-leaved plant that grows all over Europe, particularly England; for me, it is the symbol of springtime. Ramps, available in North America in farmers' markets and gourmet shops in the spring, make a good substitute.

At Frenchie's, we prepare this soup using live snow crabs, and if you can get fresh Dungeness, blue, or other crabs (about 1⅓ pounds in the shell), do try their meat in the broth.

7 ounces (200 grams) crabmeat, preferably jumbo lump

**FOR THE WILD GARLIC BROTH**
8 ounces (225 grams) wild garlic leaves or ramps
A generous handful (about 1 cup) of baby spinach leaves
Salt
Piment d'Espelette

**FOR THE GARNISH**
2 large slices sourdough bread
1½ tablespoons (21 grams) unsalted butter
1 thyme sprig
1 garlic clove, crushed
12 kalamata olives
1 small citron or lemon
1 spring onion

A handful of dill, chervil, and tarragon leaves
Juice of ⅛ lemon, or to taste
Extra virgin olive oil
Fleur de sel

## The crab
Remove any bits of shell or cartilage from the crabmeat, taking care to leave it in large pieces; refrigerate.

## The wild garlic broth
Bring a large pot of salted water to a rapid boil. Add the wild garlic leaves, bring back to a boil, and cook for 30 seconds, then add the spinach and cook for 10 more seconds. Drain in a strainer set over a bowl, then immediately transfer to a bowl of ice water to cool. Reserve about 2 cups of the cooking liquid.

Drain the greens and gently squeeze the leaves to remove as much liquid as possible. Transfer to a blender and puree, adding about 1½ cups of the reserved cooking liquid, or enough to achieve a broth consistency. Season with salt and piment d'Espelette. Refrigerate.

## The garnish
Dice the bread into ½-inch cubes. Melt the butter in a small skillet over medium heat. Add the thyme, garlic, and bread and sauté until the croutons are just golden brown, about 10 minutes. Drain on a paper towel.

Halve and pit the olives. Finely dice the citron, discarding the seeds (or grate the zest of the lemon). Peel and trim the spring onion and cut it lengthwise into very thin slices.

## Finishing touches
Roughly chop the dill, chervil, and tarragon leaves. Bring the broth to a simmer in a saucepan. Toss the crabmeat with the lemon juice in another small saucepan, add a drizzle of olive oil, and heat gently. Add the herbs and season to taste with fleur de sel.

Pour the broth into four bowls, add a spoonful of crabmeat to each one, and garnish with the croutons, olives, diced citron (or zest), and onion slices.

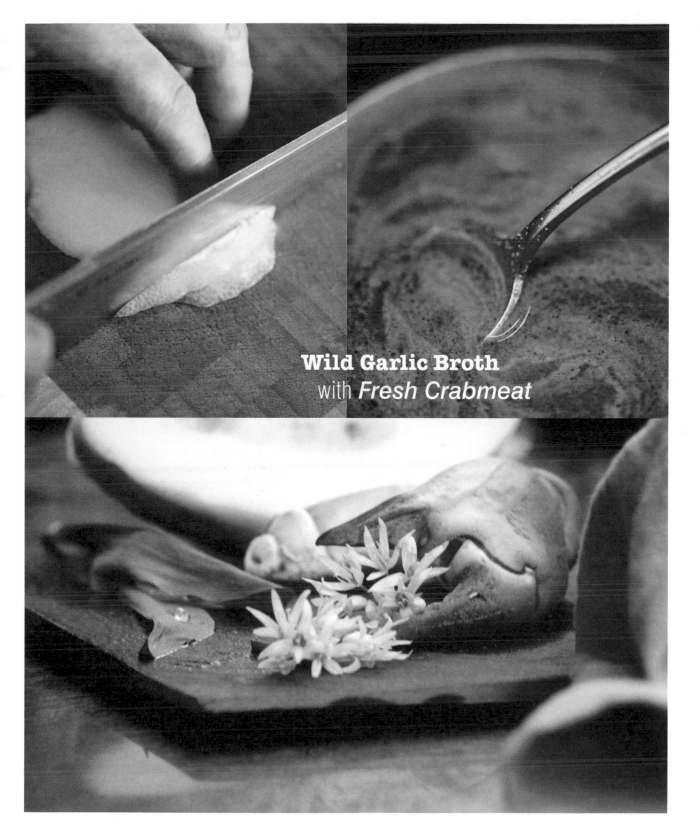

**Wild Garlic Broth** with *Fresh Crabmeat*

# Crispy Pollock *and Asparagus*
## with Vin Jaune Sauce **and Walnut Pesto**

4 servings / Wine pairing: Côtes du Jura (Savagnin); Jean-François Ganevat

Vin jaune, from the Jura, is a dry oxidized wine with notes of walnut, apple, and curry. Here the walnut pesto echoes those notes, resulting in a powerful marriage that carries the delicate flavors of the fish and the asparagus. If necessary, vin jaune can be replaced by a fino sherry to good effect.

**FOR THE VIN JAUNE SAUCE**

2 garlic cloves
2 shallots
2 tablespoons (28 grams) unsalted butter
Pinch of curry powder
Small pinch of saffron threads
Generous ¼ cup (150 ml.) vin jaune (Savagnin) or fino sherry
Juice of ½ lime, or to taste
Walnut oil
Salt

**FOR THE WALNUT PESTO**

½ cup (50 grams) walnut halves
Sunflower oil
Juice of ½ lemon, or to taste
Fine sea salt

**FOR THE ASPARAGUS**

12 ounces (340 grams) asparagus
Coarse sea salt
Olive oil

**FOR THE POLLOCK**

4 skin-on pollock (or hake or haddock) fillets, about 4 ounces (120 grams) each
Salt
Olive oil
1½ tablespoons (21 grams) unsalted butter
1 thyme sprig
1 garlic clove, crushed

¼ bunch chives, finely chopped

## The vin jaune sauce

Peel and finely chop the garlic and shallots. Melt 1 tablespoon of the butter in a small saucepan over low heat (keep the remaining butter refrigerated). Add the garlic and shallots and cook, without browning, until softened, about 5 minutes. Add the curry and saffron and cook until fragrant, about 2 minutes. Deglaze the pan with the wine, bring to a boil, and reduce by about one-third.

Transfer to a blender and blend until pureed, then add the lime juice, the remaining 1 tablespoon butter, cut into small cubes, and a drizzle of walnut oil. Season with a pinch of salt and more lime juice and/or walnut oil and set aside.

## The walnut pesto

Put the walnuts in a blender and grind them, drizzling in about 2 tablespoons sunflower oil, to a coarse puree. Season with the lemon juice and fine salt. Set aside.

## The asparagus

Cut off the woody bottoms of the asparagus on a diagonal.

Bring a large pot of salted water to a boil. Add the asparagus, bring back to a boil, and cook for 2 minutes. Drain well, transfer to a sauté pan, and drizzle with olive oil. Set aside.

## The pollock

Season the fish with salt. Heat a large nonstick frying pan over high heat. Add a drop of olive oil and place the fish skin side down in the hot pan. Cook over medium heat for 1 to 3 minutes, depending on the thickness of the fish, until you can see the sides of the fillets beginning to turn opaque. Add the butter, thyme, and crushed garlic clove and foam the butter, then turn the fish over (the skin should be nicely brown and crispy) and cook, basting the fillets with the butter, for 1 to 2 minutes, until just cooked through. Drain on a paper towel.

## Finishing touches

Add the chives to the vin jaune sauce and gently reheat the sauce, without letting it boil. Gently warm the asparagus as well.

Place a spoonful of walnut pesto in the center of each of four shallow bowls or deep plates and arrange the asparagus on top. Spoon the sauce over and top with the pollock. Serve immediately.

# Grilled Mackerel *with* Cauliflower "Farrotto" **and Trout Roe**

4 servings / Wine pairing: Burgundy white *vieilles vignes* (chardonnay); Jean-Philippe Fichet

Mackerel is one of my favorite fish. It's healthful and sustainable, but it's an oily fish that must be super-fresh and very lightly cooked to be at its best. Farro is an ancient cereal grain with earthy flavors, but when it's mixed with the cauliflower puree here, it looks like risotto. The gremolata-style garnish of citrus zest adds brightness to the dish.

**FOR THE FARROTTO**
Salt
⅝ cup (about 5 ounces/140 grams) farro, rinsed
Olive oil

**FOR THE CAULIFLOWER PUREE**
½ cauliflower
2 cups (500 ml.) whole milk, or as needed

Salt
1 small bay leaf
Juice of ¼ lemon, or to taste
¼ bunch chervil (or substitute chives), chopped

**FOR THE MACKEREL**
2 large or 4 small skin-on mackerel fillets (about 1¼ pounds/570 grams total)

Olive oil
Fleur de sel

Fleur de sel
Grated zest of 1 lemon
Grated zest of 1 lime
Grated zest of 1 orange
1 tablespoon trout roe
A handful of baby arugula
Olive oil

## The farrotto

Bring a medium pot of salted water to a boil. Add the farro and bring back to a boil, then reduce the heat and simmer, skimming off any foam, until tender, 25 to 30 minutes. Drain in a colander and cool under cold water. Transfer the farro to a bowl and toss with 1½ teaspoons olive oil. Set aside in the refrigerator.

## The cauliflower puree

Remove the core and cut the cauliflower into big chunks. Reserve 2 florets for the garnish. Put the remaining cauliflower in a medium pot and add enough milk to cover. Add a pinch of salt and the bay leaf, bring to a simmer, and cook until the cauliflower can be mashed easily between two fingers, about 20 minutes. Drain the cauliflower in a sieve set over a bowl; reserve the cooking liquid. Remove the bay leaf.

Transfer the cauliflower to a food processor and process, adding enough of the cooking liquid (about ⅓ cup) to obtain a smooth, creamy puree. Season with the lemon juice and salt. Set aside. Reserve the remaining cooking liquid.

## The mackerel

Fire up an outdoor grill or heat a ridged grill pan over medium-high heat. Lightly massage the skin side of the mackerel fillets with olive oil. Season with fleur de sel and place them skin side down on the hot grill or pan. Cook for about 2 minutes, just until the fillets have started to turn opaque, then turn them, cook for about 5 seconds, just until cooked through, and remove from the heat.

## Finishing touches

Meanwhile, combine the farro and cauliflower puree in a large saucepan and heat gently over low heat until hot, adding more of the reserved cooking liquid if necessary. Season to taste with salt and a dash more lemon juice and stir in the chervil.

Divide the farrotto among four plates. Arrange the mackerel fillets on top and sprinkle with fleur de sel, the citrus zests, and the trout roe. Garnish with the arugula, lightly tossed with olive oil, and, finally, grate the reserved raw cauliflower florets over the plates.

**Grilled Mackerel** *with* Cauliflower "Farrotto" **and Trout Roe**

# Grilled **Baby Lamb** with **Fava Beans,** Sweet Peas, *and* **Mint Chutney**

4 servings / Wine pairing: Crozes-Hermitage red (Syrah); David Reynaud

This is a reminder of my time at The Savoy Grill in London, where we cooked all sorts of typical British dishes. I love mint with lamb, but I am not crazy about the traditional mint sauce, which is both too sweet and too acidic for my taste. With the help of my Indian apprentice Gaurav, who shared his chutney recipe with me, I revisited and personalized this British classic.

**FOR THE LAMB**
1 rosemary sprig
2 garlic cloves, crushed
Grated zest of 1 lemon
1 teaspoon crushed black pepper
2 tablespoons olive oil
4 pieces boneless lamb leg or loin
   (about 8 ounces/225 grams each)
Salt and freshly ground black pepper

**FOR THE VEGETABLE GARNISH**
16 tiny new potatoes
Coarse sea salt
Olive oil
1¼ pounds (600 grams) sweet peas
   in the pod (about 1 cup/160 grams
   shelled peas)
1¼ pounds (600 grams) fava beans
   in the pod (about 1 cup/160 grams
   shelled favas)

**FOR THE MINT CHUTNEY**
½ teaspoon cumin seeds

1 small green mango
1 bunch mint
½ bunch cilantro
Extra virgin olive oil
Salt

2 tablespoons (28 grams) unsalted
   butter
Piment d'Espelette
Salt
Fleur de sel
Crushed black pepper

## The lamb marinade

Combine the rosemary, garlic, lemon zest, crushed pepper, and olive oil in a baking dish. Add the lamb, turning to coat and rubbing the marinade into the meat. Cover and marinate for at least 4 hours in the refrigerator.

## The vegetable garnish

Meanwhile, put the potatoes in a large pot of cold salted water, bring to a boil, and cook for about 15 minutes, until tender: the tip of a knife should enter the flesh without resistance. Drain the potatoes thoroughly, transfer to a bowl, and add a drizzle of olive oil. Set aside at room temperature.

Shell the peas and refrigerate. Shell the fava beans.

Bring a medium pot of salted water to a boil. Blanch the fava beans in the boiling water for 30 seconds, then drain and immediately transfer to a bowl of ice water to cool. Drain again and peel off the outer skin. Refrigerate.

## The mint chutney

Toast the cumin seeds in a dry skillet over low heat until fragrant, about 3 minutes; be careful not to burn them.

Peel and pit the mango and cut enough of the flesh into ½-inch dice to make ⅓ cup (the green mango will bring acidity to the chutney without darkening its bright green color); reserve the remaining mango for another use. Remove the leaves from the mint and cilantro stems.

Combine the cumin, mango, and herbs in a blender and blend until finely chopped, while drizzling in about 2½ tablespoons olive oil. Season with salt and refrigerate.

## Cooking the lamb

Remove the lamb from the refrigerator about 1 hour before cooking. Fire up an outdoor grill.

Season the lamb with salt and pepper and grill it for about 5 minutes or so on each side, depending on the thickness:

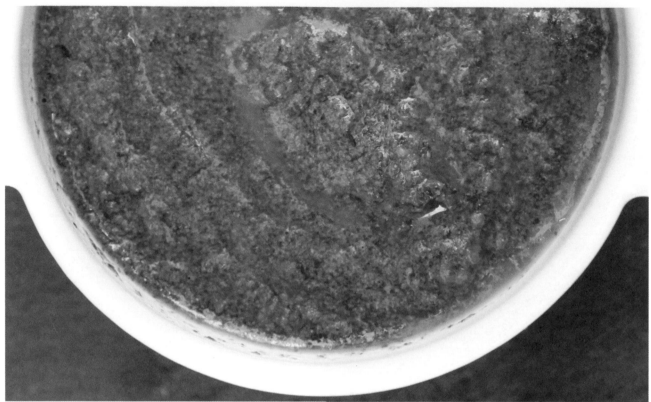

when blood starts to bead up on the surface, the lamb will be cooked to medium-rare. Transfer to a plate and let rest for 10 minutes.

## Finishing touches

Meanwhile, melt the butter in a large skillet over low heat. Add the peas and cook for 1 minute, then add the potatoes and favas and heat, stirring and tossing the vegetables, until the potatoes are warmed through. Remove from the heat and toss with 1 tablespoon of the chutney. Add a pinch of piment d'Espelette and season with salt to taste.

For the most tender meat, slice the lamb crosswise against the grain (see the photo opposite).

Divide the vegetables among four plates and add a spoonful of mint chutney to each plate. Arrange the meat alongside and season it with fleur de sel and crushed black pepper.

*Grilled* **Baby Lamb**
*with* **Fava Beans,** Sweet Peas,
*and* **Mint Chutney**

# Blue Cheese, Lemon Zest,
## *and* Amarena Cherries

**4 servings / Wine pairing: Canadian ice cider (apple ice wine)**

This is one of our signature "cheese dessert" plates. Amarena cherries are small dark Italian sour cherries that are sold preserved in syrup. Sweet and fragrant, they are most often used in desserts, but they are wonderful with a strong blue cheese, rounding it out and adding both softness and tartness.

**About 12 ounces (340 grams) blue cheese, such as bleu des Causses, Fourme d'Ambert, Gorgonzola, or Stilton**

**Grated zest of 1 lemon**
**A handful of tiny basil leaves**

**24 to 30 jarred Amarena cherries**

Take the cheese out of the refrigerator at least 2 hours before serving to bring it to room temperature.

Break the cheese into large chunks and divide among four salad plates or small wooden boards. Sprinkle with the lemon zest and basil leaves. Serve with the cherries.

# *Strawberries,* **Poached Rhubarb,** and **Shortbread Cookies**

4 servings / Wine pairing: Bugey-Cerdon sparkling rosé (Poulsard, Gamay); Philippe Balivet

In France, I use small, sweet, and fragrant Gariguette strawberries. In the States, look for Tristar strawberries or other ripe, sweet berries at the farmers' market. A whipped cream canister will help make the cream extra light and fluffy, but it is not required.

**FOR THE SHORTBREAD COOKIES**
1¾ cups (255 grams) pastry or cake flour
½ cup plus 2 tablespoons (85 grams) fine semolina
1 vanilla bean
½ cup plus 1 tablespoon (115 grams) granulated sugar
½ pound (2 sticks/225 grams) unsalted butter, at room temperature
Grated zest of 1 lemon

**FOR THE POACHED RHUBARB**
2 red rhubarb stalks
¾ cup (150 grams) granulated sugar
⅔ cup (150 ml.) water
½ vanilla bean
4 verbena leaves or 1 tablespoon dried verbena (or substitute the grated zest of 1 lemon)

**FOR THE STRAWBERRIES**
8 ounces (230 grams) small ripe strawberries
¼ cup (50 grams) granulated sugar

**FOR THE WHIPPED CREAM**
½ vanilla bean
1 cup (200 ml.) very cold heavy cream
2 tablespoons confectioners' sugar

## The shortbread cookies

Whisk together the flour and semolina in a bowl. With the tip of a sharp paring knife, split the vanilla bean lengthwise and scrape out the seeds (reserve the pod for another use).

Combine the sugar and butter in a large bowl and beat with an electric mixer until light and fluffy. Beat in the vanilla seeds and lemon zest. On low speed, beat in the flour mixture, in 2 additions, just until incorporated; do not overwork.

Turn the dough out, form it into a thick disk, and wrap in plastic wrap. Refrigerate for 30 minutes.

Preheat the oven to 300°F. Line two baking sheets with parchment paper.

On a lightly floured surface, roll the dough out to ½ inch thick. Prick it all over with a fork. With a cookie cutter, cut the dough into 1½-inch rounds and place them 1 inch apart on the lined sheets. Bake for 20 to 23 minutes, until the edges are golden brown. Let cool on the pans for at least 10 minutes, then transfer to a rack to cool completely.

## The poached rhubarb

Cut the rhubarb into 1½-inch-long sections. Combine the sugar, water, split vanilla bean, and verbena in a small pot and bring to a boil. Add the rhubarb. As soon as the liquid returns to a boil, transfer the rhubarb and its cooking syrup to a bowl or other container; make sure the rhubarb is completely submerged. Let cool, then cover and refrigerate.

## The strawberries

Wash and hull the strawberries, cut them lengthwise in half, and transfer to a bowl. Add the sugar, toss gently, and set aside to macerate for at least 30 minutes.

## The whipped cream

Meanwhile, split the vanilla bean and remove the seeds. Whip the cream with the sugar and vanilla seeds in a bowl just to soft peaks. Cover and refrigerate.

## To serve

Spoon the rhubarb, with its syrup, into shallow bowls. Using a slotted spoon, add the strawberries, and top with the whipped cream. Finish with a drizzle of strawberry syrup and serve with the shortbread cookies.

*Strawberries,* **Poached Rhubarb,** and **Shortbread Cookies**

# summer

# *Watermelon,* **Ricotta Salata,** Mint, **and Pine Nut Salad**

**4 servings / Wine pairing: Rosé Champagne (Pinot Noir, Pinot Meunier); Franck Pascal**

This can be a starter, a dessert, or a great hors d'oeuvre: just add toothpicks! The salty ricotta salata brings the seasoning to the dish, balancing the sweetness of the watermelon.

At the restaurant, we place the watermelon in a sous-vide bag and compress it under the highest pressure, which gives the watermelon the dense meaty texture and bright color shown in the photograph (opposite). If you have a vacuum-pack machine, you can try this. However, the dish is outstanding even when simply prepared as directed below.

**FOR THE WATERMELON**
1 mini seedless watermelon
   (about 4 pounds/1.75 kg.)
1 teaspoon unsalted butter
2 tablespoons pine nuts

**FOR THE CHILE OIL**
1 small red chile pepper
2 tablespoons olive oil

A chunk of ricotta salata
   (about 3 ounces/85 grams)
2 mint sprigs
Fleur de sel

## The watermelon

Cut off both ends of the watermelon, then cut it into a rectangular shape, removing all the rind. Cut it into 1-inch cubes and refrigerate.

Melt the butter in a small skillet over low heat. Add the pine nuts and toast, stirring frequently, until lightly golden, about 5 minutes. Drain on a paper towel.

## The chile oil

Cut the chile lengthwise in half, remove the seeds, and slice into a very fine julienne (matchsticks). Put in a small bowl and cover with the oil. Let infuse at room temperature for at least 30 minutes.

## Finishing touches

Using a vegetable peeler, cut thin shavings of ricotta from the chunk of cheese. Remove the mint leaves from the stems.

Place 5 or more cubes of watermelon on each plate and season with fleur de sel. Scatter the pine nuts, mint leaves, and ricotta shavings over the top and drizzle with the chile oil.

# Heirloom Tomato *and* Red Currant Salad
## *with Basil* and Croutons

**4 servings / Wine pairing: Austrian Riesling; Kamptal Loimer**

This summer dish is based on panzanella, the traditional Italian salad of tomatoes and stale bread. It's *cocina povera* at its best—with the contemporary addition of tomato water, a technique I learned at Gramercy Tavern.

Note that you need to start the tomato water a day ahead.

**FOR THE TOMATO WATER**
2 shallots
½ bunch cilantro
½ bunch basil
2 pounds (1 kg.) ripe tomatoes
Dash of sherry vinegar
Dash of white balsamic vinegar
1 teaspoon salt

**FOR THE CROUTONS**
½ small sourdough bread
  (about 4 ounces/115 grams)
Olive oil
1 tablespoon (14 grams) unsalted butter
1 thyme sprig
1 garlic clove, smashed

16 fresh almonds in the shell
  (or substitute Marcona almonds)
4 ounces (125 grams) red currants
  (or substitute 1 cup raspberries)
2 pounds (1 kg.) heirloom tomatoes of
  different varieties and colors
16 basil leaves
Fleur de sel
Extra virgin olive oil

## The tomato water

One day ahead, peel and mince the shallots. Remove the leaves from the cilantro and basil. Cut the tomatoes into quarters. Combine the tomatoes, shallots, herbs, and vinegars in a bowl and, using an immersion blender, blend to a coarse puree (or use a regular blender). Season with the salt and marinate in the refrigerator overnight.

The next day, set a sieve lined with cheesecloth or a coffee filter over a bowl. Pour in the tomato mixture and allow to stand until the clear tomato water drains into the bowl, at least 30 minutes.

## The croutons

Meanwhile, preheat the oven to 350°F.

With a serrated knife, remove the crust from the bread, then cut the bread into ¾-inch cubes. Heat a large skillet over medium heat. Add about 1 teaspoon olive oil and the butter. When the butter begins to foam, toss in the thyme, garlic, and bread cubes and fry the cubes, turning often, until nicely golden, about 6 minutes.

Transfer the croutons to a baking sheet and toast in the oven until crisp, 8 to 10 minutes. Drain on paper towels.

## Finishing touches

If using fresh almonds, crack the almonds open with a small knife (rather than a nutcracker, which would break the nuts) and peel off the yellow outer skin. Remove the currants from the stems.

Cut the heirloom tomatoes into big irregular chunks. Put them in a salad bowl and gently toss with the currants, basil leaves, and croutons. Add some or all of the tomato water as desired (see the photo at top right), season with fleur de sel, and toss again. Divide among four shallow bowls or plates. Sprinkle with the almonds, drizzle with olive oil, and serve immediately.

**Heirloom Tomato** *and*
**Red Currant Salad**
*with Basil* and Croutons

# Fresh Tagliatelle
## with **Chanterelles** and Lemon Zest

4 servings / Wine pairing: Saint-Joseph white (Marsanne, Roussane); Pierre Gonon

This beautiful plate of pasta combines the earthiness of mushrooms, the acidity of lemon, and the delicate tang of thick crème fraîche. It's easy but hugely rewarding to make your own pasta.

**FOR THE PASTA DOUGH**
1½ cups (200 grams) Italian "00" flour
¾ cup (100 grams) pastry or cake flour
Pinch of fine salt
2 extra-large eggs
3 extra-large egg yolks

**FOR THE MUSHROOMS**
9 ounces (250 grams) small
    chanterelles
½ bunch flat-leaf parsley
1½ tablespoons (21 grams) unsalted
    butter
Salt
2 tablespoons coarse sea salt

¼ cup (60 grams) crème fraîche
Grated zest and juice of 1 lemon
Generous ½ cup (80 grams) freshly
    grated Parmesan

Generous handful of baby arugula
Olive oil
Fleur de sel

## The pasta dough

Combine the flours and salt in a large bowl and make a well in the center. Lightly beat the eggs with a fork in a small bowl, then beat in the yolks. Pour the egg mixture into the flour "well" and gradually stir in the flour with a fork; when the dough becomes too stiff to stir, mix and knead in the remaining flour with your hands. Turn the dough out onto a floured surface and knead it until it comes together into a ball. Wrap in plastic wrap and let rest in the refrigerator for at least 1 hour.

## The tagliatelle

Divide the dough into 3 pieces. With a rolling pin (or your palms), flatten each one to ½ inch thick. Roll one piece through the pasta machine on the widest setting. Fold the dough in half or into thirds and pass it through the same setting, then repeat several times, until it's smooth and silky. Lower the setting and again pass the dough through the machine, sprinkling the dough with flour if it becomes sticky. Repeat until you have rolled the dough through the next-to-the-last setting. Lay the sheet of dough on a floured surface and repeat with the remaining dough.

Cut the pasta into 8-inch-long sheets, then use the fettuccine cutter on the pasta machine to cut the sheets into ¼-inch-wide ribbons. Toss with a little flour and spread out on a floured baking sheet to dry at room temperature (refrigerate if not using the same day).

## The mushrooms

Trim the chanterelles and scrape clean with a damp cloth and/or the tip of a small knife. (If they are very dirty, wash them very quickly in cold water, then immediately drain on a kitchen towel and pat dry.) If your chanterelles are large, halve or quarter them.

Remove the parsley leaves from the stems.

## Cooking the pasta

Bring a large pot of water to a boil.

Meanwhile, heat the butter in a large skillet over medium-high heat until foaming. Add the chanterelles and sauté until tender, 5 to 8 minutes. Season with a pinch of salt and set aside in a warm spot.

When the water is boiling, add the coarse salt, then add the tagliatelle and cook until al dente, about 2 minutes. Drain, reserving a little of the pasta water, and transfer the pasta to the pan with the mushrooms.

Add the crème fraîche, parsley leaves, lemon zest, half of the lemon juice, and three-quarters of the Parmesan. Stir well, adding a little of the reserved pasta water if necessary, and season with salt.

## Finishing touches

Toss the arugula with a drizzle of olive oil, the rest of the lemon juice, and a pinch of fleur de sel.

Divide the arugula among four shallow bowls and top with the pasta. Sprinkle with the rest of the Parmesan and serve immediately.

**Fresh Tagliatelle** with **Chanterelles** and Lemon Zest

# Smoked Trout with *Avocado Puree* and **Marinated Cucumbers**

4 servings / Wine pairing: Old Muscadet de Sèvre-et-Maine sur Lie (Melon de Bourgogne); Domaine de Fay d'Homme

Smoking fish at home is actually quite easy if you have an inexpensive stovetop smoker, and the result is gently cooked fish with a very delicate smoky flavor—far more subtle than any you can buy. I love the way the yogurt and avocado lighten the fattiness of the fish, and the combination of its smokiness and the acidity you get from the pickled onions and marinated cucumbers.

**EQUIPMENT**
A stovetop smoker
Beechwood or other smoking chips

**FOR THE PICKLED ONIONS**
⅔ cup (150 ml.) white wine vinegar
  or rice vinegar
Scant ¼ cup (50 ml.) water
¼ cup (50 grams) sugar
1 tablespoon kosher salt
1 small beet
1 small red onion or other
  sweet onion

**FOR THE AVOCADO PUREE**
1 ripe avocado
Generous ½ cup (125 grams)
  Greek yogurt
Juice of ½ lemon, or to taste
Avocado oil or olive oil
Salt

**FOR THE MARINATED CUCUMBERS**
2 to 3 small cucumbers, such as gherkin
  or kirby
1 tablespoon coarse sea salt
½ teaspoon granulated sugar

**FOR THE SMOKED TROUT**
4 fresh trout fillets
Fleur de sel
Olive oil

White wine vinegar
Olive oil
Piment d'Espelette
Leaves from 2 or 3 dill sprigs
Fleur de sel
Borage flowers (optional)

## The pickled onions

To make the pickling juice, combine the vinegar, water, sugar, kosher salt, and beet in a small nonreactive saucepan and bring to a boil, stirring to dissolve the sugar.

Meanwhile, slice the onion very fine (¹⁄₁₀ inch thick or less) with a mandoline and put the slices in a small deep bowl. Pour the pickling juice, with the beet, over the onions (the beet will tint the onions pink), and let cool to room temperature, then refrigerate. (The onions will keep for at least 5 days in the refrigerator.)

## The avocado puree

Peel, pit, and dice the avocado. Transfer to a blender, add the yogurt, lemon juice, a drizzle of oil, and a pinch of salt, and puree. Transfer to a small bowl, cover, and refrigerate.

## The marinated cucumbers

Cut off both ends of the cucumbers. With the mandoline, slice them lengthwise into strips, about ¹⁄₁₀ inch thick; you need 12 slices for this dish (discard the first and last slices from each cucumber). Toss with the coarse salt and sugar, arrange on a large deep plate, and let marinate for 20 minutes.

Carefully rinse the cucumbers with cold water and pat dry with paper towels. Reserve in the refrigerator.

## The smoked trout

Set up the smoker with the wood chips as directed by the manufacturer.

Season the skin side of the trout fillets with fleur de sel and a drizzle of olive oil.

When smoke starts coming out of the smoker, place the trout fillets skin side down on the rack, cover, and smoke for 3 to 5 minutes, until the trout is just cooked. Transfer the fillets to a plate and carefully remove the skin.

## Finishing touches

Put the cucumber strips in a bowl and gently toss with a dash of white wine vinegar, a drizzle of olive oil, a pinch of piment d'Espelette, and most of the dill, reserving some for the garnish. Season to taste with fleur de sel if necessary.

Spread some of the avocado puree across the center of each plate. Top with the trout fillets and sprinkle with fleur de sel. Roll up 12 of the cucumber strips and place 3 rolls seam side down on each fillet. Top each cucumber roll with a pickled onion slice. Garnish with borage flowers, if using, and the remaining dill.

**Smoked Trout** *with* Avocado Puree *and* **Marinated Cucumbers**

# Brined Chicken with
# Roasted Zucchini and Tapenade

4 servings / Wine pairing: White Rioja (Viura grape); Olivier Rivière

Inspired by Mediterranean home cooking, this is a light, fresh dish with intense flavors (from the brine, tapenade, and herbs). It is essential to get organic free-range chicken and to cook it with its skin until crisp. The chicken breast shown in the photograph (opposite) is boned but with the wing bone left intact, a cut sometimes called a *suprême*; these are readily available in France but less so in North America, although you may find a butcher who can prepare them. If possible, have the butcher cut up a whole small chicken for you; if not, you may have to order skin-on boneless breasts and thighs.

Note that the brining time is 4 hours.

**FOR THE BRINE**
1¼ cups (295 grams) water
⅓ cup (75 ml.) white wine vinegar
Scant ¾ cup (125 grams) granulated
   sugar
6 tablespoons (100 grams) fine sea salt
1 teaspoon mustard seeds
2 garlic cloves, crushed
1 bunch thyme (reserve 1 sprig for the
   zucchini and 1 for cooking the chicken)

**FOR THE CHICKEN**
2 skin-on boneless free-range chicken
   breasts (see the headnote)
2 skin-on boneless free-range chicken
   thighs

1 tablespoon grapeseed oil
1 tablespoon (14 grams) unsalted butter
1 garlic clove, crushed
1 thyme sprig (from above)
1 rosemary sprig

**FOR THE ROASTED ZUCCHINI**
2 pounds (1 kg.) mixed zucchini, such as
   green, yellow, and round
Olive oil
Fleur de sel
Piment d'Espelette
1 thyme sprig (from above)

**FOR THE TAPENADE**
Generous ½ cup (100 grams) unpitted
   black olives, such as Kalamata
Juice of ½ lemon, or to taste
Olive oil

**FOR THE BROWN BUTTER
VINAIGRETTE**
2 tablespoons (28 grams) unsalted butter
Juice of ½ lemon, or to taste
Fine sea salt

**FOR THE GARNISH**
Leaves from ⅓ bunch tarragon
Leaves from ⅓ bunch dill
Leaves from ⅓ bunch chervil

## The brine

Combine the water, vinegar, sugar, salt, mustard seeds, garlic, and thyme (reserving 2 sprigs) in a medium nonreactive saucepan and bring to a boil, stirring to dissolve the sugar and salt. Let cool, then refrigerate until cold.

## Brining the chicken

Put the chicken in a large deep bowl. Add the brine, making sure the chicken is submerged, and refrigerate for 4 hours.

Drain the chicken, rinse under cold water, and pat dry with paper towels. Refrigerate.

## The roasted zucchini

Meanwhile, preheat the oven to 350°F.

Cut the zucchini into slices about ½ inch thick. Put the zucchini on a baking sheet lined with parchment paper and toss with a drizzle of olive oil. Season with fleur de sel and piment d'Espelette and spread out on the baking sheet. Add the sprig of thyme.

Roast the zucchini for 15 to 20 minutes, until just tender. Set aside.

## The tapenade

Halve and pit the olives (I prefer to buy unpitted olives and pit them myself, since they are much more flavorful). Transfer to a blender, add the lemon juice and a dash of olive oil, and blend until smooth. Transfer to a small bowl and set aside.

## The brown butter vinaigrette

Heat the butter in a small saucepan over medium heat until it is brown and smells nutty (in French, this is *beurre noisette*, hazelnut butter). Strain through a fine sieve or cheesecloth into a small bowl. Whisk in the lemon juice and a pinch of salt. Set aside in a warm spot.

## The chicken

Meanwhile, 30 minutes before cooking, take the chicken out of the refrigerator and pat dry. (Do not season it—the salty brine took care of that.)

Heat a very large skillet over medium-high heat until hot, then add the grapeseed oil and heat until hot. Add the chicken pieces, skin side down, reduce the heat to medium, and cook for 12 minutes, or until the chicken is almost cooked through (lower the heat slightly if necessary). Add the butter, garlic, thyme, and rosemary to the pan. Once the butter is foaming, turn the chicken pieces over and cook, basting the skin with the butter, until cooked through, about 2 minutes for the thighs and 6 minutes for the breasts. As the chicken is done, transfer it to a plate.

Let the chicken rest for 5 to 10 minutes.

## To serve

Cut each piece of chicken in half.

With a rubber spatula, spread a spoonful of tapenade on each plate. Arrange some of the roasted zucchini and one piece of breast and one piece of thigh on each plate. Toss the herbs with the vinaigrette (if it has thickened, rewarm it briefly over low heat), then scatter the herb salad over the plates and serve.

Brined Chicken with
Roasted Zucchini and Tapenade

# Grilled Rib-Eye Steak *and Potatoes-in-a-Bag*
## with Anchovy and Rosemary Vinaigrette

6 servings / Wine pairing: Sicilian Nero d'Avola; Arianna Occhipinti

I love pairing anchovies with beef or lamb; they bring a great kick to the meat. It's best to use salt-packed anchovies rather than oil-preserved ones, since they have much more flavor. Cooking the potatoes in the embers is an unusual but hassle-free technique that results in soft, moist flesh.

**EQUIPMENT**
Parchment paper
Mortar and pestle

**FOR THE POTATOES**
1¼ pounds (800 grams) small potatoes,
   such as fingerlings
1 large red onion
24 cherry or grape tomatoes
1 rosemary sprig

Grated zest of 1 lemon
Fleur de sel
Freshly ground black pepper
Olive oil

**FOR THE ANCHOVY AND ROSEMARY
VINAIGRETTE**
3 salt-packed anchovies
1 small rosemary sprig
Fleur de sel

Juice of ½ lemon
Olive oil

**FOR THE BEEF**
1 bone-in beef rib-eye steak,
   3 to 4 pounds (1.4 to 1.8 kg.)
Fleur de sel
Crushed black pepper

## The potatoes

Cut the potatoes into scant ¼-inch-thick slices. Peel and mince the red onion. Remove the rosemary leaves from the stem.

Combine the potatoes, onion, cherry tomatoes, and rosemary in a large bowl. Add the lemon zest, a generous pinch of fleur de sel, and pepper to taste and toss with a drizzle of olive oil.

Lay a 12-by-24-inch sheet of parchment paper on a work surface. Fold it crosswise in half, then open it out. Arrange half the vegetables on one side, leaving a border on the 3 open sides, then fold the paper over and seal the 3 open sides securely, folding and crimping them over themselves several times. Wrap the bag in three 12-by-24-inch sheets of foil (or 2 sheets, if you will be cooking the potatoes in the oven). Repeat to make a second package of vegetables.

## The anchovy and rosemary vinaigrette

Rinse the anchovies under cold water to remove the salt. Remove the 2 fillets from each anchovy, pat them dry, and coarsely chop them.

Remove the rosemary leaves from the stem and finely chop, then crush with a pinch of fleur de sel in a mortar to a coarse paste. Add the anchovies and lemon juice, mashing the anchovies with the pestle, then stir in a drizzle of olive oil to emulsify. Transfer to a small serving bowl.

## The beef

Fire up an outdoor girl. (If using a gas grill, preheat the oven to 350°F.)

Generously season the beef on both sides with fleur de sel and crushed pepper. Grill the beef over a medium-hot fire for 8 to 12 minutes, depending on the thickness of the meat.

Carefully lift up the grill and place the potatoes-in-a-bag in the coals. (Or put the bags on a baking sheet, slide into the oven, and cook for 20 to 25 minutes; check with the tip of a knife as described below.) Turn the beef over and grill it on the other side for another 8 to 12 minutes: when the first beads of blood appear on the surface, the meat will be cooked to medium-rare. Transfer the meat to a rack or plate and let rest for about 15 minutes.

Meanwhile, after they have cooked for 20 minutes, take one packet of potatoes out of the embers and check the doneness with the tip of a knife (inserted through the foil and paper). When they are ready, transfer the potatoes to a serving bowl.

## To serve

Carve the meat and season each slice with a little bit of fleur de sel and crushed pepper. Serve with the potatoes and vinaigrette on the side.

**Grilled Rib-Eye Steak** *and Potatoes-in-a-Bag* **with Anchovy** and Rosemary Vinaigrette

# Fresh Peaches, Smoked Mozzarella,
## and *Aged Balsamic*

**4 servings / Wine pairing: Languedoc white (Viognier); Pierre Vaïsse**

A straightforward dish that can be served as an appetizer or a combination dessert/cheese course. Tearing the peaches apart, rather than cutting them, gives them an appealingly rustic look and also allows the flavors to penetrate the flesh better. I love the layer of smokiness from the smoked mozzarella, but you can use fresh mozzarella or creamy burrata.

2 basil sprigs
2 purple basil sprigs
4 ripe, juicy peaches
Fleur de sel

About 2 tablespoons olive oil
1 ball smoked mozzarella
(about 1 pound/450 grams)

Crushed black pepper
About 1 tablespoon aged balsamic
vinegar

Remove the leaves from the basil stems. Halve the peaches and remove the pits. Tear the peaches into big irregular pieces and put them in a bowl. Toss with the basil leaves, a pinch or two of fleur de sel, and a drizzle of olive oil.

Cut the mozzarella into 4 wedges and place in four shallow bowls. Season with fleur de sel and crushed pepper and drizzle with olive oil. Garnish with the peaches and basil leaves and finish with a dash of balsamic.

# Bittersweet Chocolate and *Wild Strawberry* Tart

8 servings / Wine pairing: Red Pineau des Charentes; Domaine Château de Beaulon, or a good sherry

Wild strawberries, *fraises des bois*, are a rare delicacy that form a magical alliance with the intensity of bittersweet chocolate. If you cannot find them, choose the smallest, most fragrant strawberries at your farmers' market.

**EQUIPMENT**
A 10-inch fluted tart pan with
 a removable bottom
Dried beans or pie weights

**FOR THE SWEET TART DOUGH**
8 tablespoons (1 stick/113 grams)
 cold unsalted butter
1¼ cups plus 5 tablespoons (175 grams)
 all-purpose flour
⅓ cup (66 grams) pastry or cake flour

2½ tablespoons (25 grams) almond flour
 (finely ground almonds)
¾ cup (72 grams) confectioners' sugar
1½ teaspoons fine sea salt
1 large egg, at room temperature

1 egg, beaten, for egg wash

**FOR THE CHOCOLATE FILLING**
6 ounces (170 grams)
 70% bittersweet chocolate

1 cup (237 ml.) heavy cream
½ cup (118 ml.) whole milk
2 tablespoons granulated sugar
1 small egg

**FOR THE GARNISH**
8 ounces (225 grams) wild strawberries
 (see the headnote)
Fleur de sel
Olive oil

## The dough

Cut the butter into small pieces. Whisk the flours, almond flour, sugar, and salt together in a medium bowl. With your fingertips, work in the butter until the texture is sandy. Quickly beat the egg with a fork in a small bowl, then add to the butter mixture and mix with your hands until the dough just comes together. Flatten the dough into a disk, wrap in plastic wrap, and chill for 2 hours.

Put the dough on a large sheet of plastic wrap or wax paper, cover it with another sheet, and roll it into a 12-inch circle. Lift off the top sheet of plastic wrap and carefully invert the dough into the tart pan. Lift off the second sheet and gently press the dough into the bottom and up the sides of the pan, then cut off the excess by running the rolling pin over the edge. (The dough is fragile, but any tears can be patched easily.) Chill for 30 minutes to 1 hour.

## The tart shell

Preheat the oven to 325°F.

Cut out a parchment paper circle (see the photos on page 74) and line the tart shell with the parchment. Fill with dried beans or pie weights and bake for 20 minutes. Remove the beans and paper and bake for 5 more minutes.

Brush the tart shell all over with the egg wash. Bake for 5 to 7 minutes longer, until golden brown. Let cool to room temperature. Reduce the oven temperature to 300°F.

## The chocolate filling

Finely chop the chocolate and put it in a bowl. Combine the cream, milk, and sugar in a medium saucepan and bring to a boil, stirring to dissolve the sugar. Pour the boiling liquid over the chopped chocolate and let stand for 30 seconds, then mix with a rubber spatula until the mixture is smooth. Let cool to lukewarm, then mix in the egg.

Pour the filling into the baked tart shell and bake for 25 to 30 minutes. The tart is done when the filling is just set. If you shake the pan gently, the chocolate mass should move in one block. Let the tart cool to room temperature on a rack. Do not put it in the refrigerator! This tart should be served at room temperature on the day it is made.

## Finishing touches

Unmold the tart. Arrange the strawberries on top of the tart (if using bigger strawberries, cut them into halves or quarters). Sprinkle with fleur de sel and add a dash of olive oil.

Bittersweet Chocolate and *Wild Strawberry* **Tart**

# fall

# **Spanish Ham,** Corn, Bell Peppers, and *Kaffir Lime*

4 servings / Wine pairing: Italian beer, such as Birra del Borgo blonde, or a good lager beer

A back-from-the-holidays dish, inspired by Mexican flavors. The weather is still warm, and corn is extra sweet. This can be eaten as an appetizer or as a side dish—for a roast pig, perhaps, or any grilled meat. I like the fresh Asian touch of fragrant kaffir lime, but the recipe also works well with regular lime zest. As for the pickled ginger, it is one of my go-to ingredients: it adds zing to anything! I use the pickling liquid like vinegar, to season raw fish dishes, such as crudo or ceviche, or a sauce for a pork dish.

If you can't find Spanish ham, you can substitute good prosciutto or even culatello.

**FOR THE PICKLED GINGER**
Scant 2 ounces (50 grams) fresh ginger
⅔ cup (150 ml.) rice vinegar
¼ cup (50 ml.) water
¼ cup (50 grams) granulated sugar
¼ teaspoon salt

**FOR THE GARNISH**
2 medium red bell peppers
Olive oil
Fine sea salt
2 ears corn
¼ bunch cilantro
2 small shallots

2 tablespoons (28 grams) unsalted butter
Olive oil
Grated zest of ¼ lime, preferably kaffir
    lime
Juice of ½ lime, or to taste
Fleur de sel
3 ounces (85 grams) thinly sliced
    Spanish ham

## The pickled ginger
Peel the ginger and slice it very thin with a mandoline. Put it in a small bowl.

Combine the rice vinegar, water, sugar, and salt in a small nonreactive saucepan and bring to a boil, stirring to dissolve the sugar and salt. Pour the liquid over the ginger and let cool to room temperature, then cover tightly and refrigerate. (The ginger will keep for weeks.)

## The garnish
Rub the bell peppers with olive oil, coating the peppers evenly, and sprinkle with salt. Grill them over a flame, either on an outdoor grill or directly over a gas burner, turning occasionally, until evenly blackened. Put the peppers in a bowl and cover tightly with plastic wrap, so that the steam helps loosen the skin. Let stand for 20 minutes.

Meanwhile, husk the corn and cut off the kernels. Remove the cilantro leaves from the stems and coarsely chop. Peel and finely dice the shallots. Chop enough drained pickled ginger to make 1 tablespoon.

Peel off the charred skin from the peppers, remove the cores and seeds, and slice the peppers into thin strips.

## Finishing touches
Melt the butter with a drizzle of olive oil in a large skillet over medium heat. Add the corn and cook over medium-low heat until tender but still crisp, 3 to 4 minutes. Add the shallots, pepper strips, and chopped pickled ginger and cook until the shallots are softened, just a few minutes. Add 2 tablespoons of the pickled ginger juice, the lime zest, juice, and chopped cilantro and stir well; taste and add more ginger juice and/or lime juice if desired. Season to taste with fleur de sel.

Divide among four plates, top with the ham, and serve immediately.

**Spanish Ham,** Corn,
Bell Peppers,
and *Kaffir Lime*

# Sautéed Wild Mushrooms with Grapes and Aged Mimolette

4 servings / Wine pairing: Arbois vin jaune (Savagnin); Stéphane Tissot

Combining earthy and nutty flavors, this dish is the quintessence of autumn.
You can use any wild mushrooms you may find in the farmers' market. Mimolette
is an orange cow's-milk cheese from the north of France that becomes very firm
when aged; aged cheddar, or any nutty-flavored mature cheese, can be substituted.

12 ounces (320 grams) wild mushrooms, such as chanterelles, yellow-foot chanterelles, hedgehog, porcini, and/or blewits

**FOR THE YOGURT-HAZELNUT SAUCE**
½ cup (125 ml.) plain full-fat yogurt
1 tablespoon chopped skinned hazelnuts
2 teaspoons freshly grated Parmesan

2 tablespoons herb leaves, such as tarragon, dill, and/or flat-leaf parsley
Hazelnut oil
Salt

**FOR THE GARNISH**
2 tablespoons skinned hazelnuts
Salt
A small bunch of Muscat or black seedless grapes (about 24 grapes)

2 ounces (57 grams) aged Mimolette or aged cheddar
3 tarragon sprigs

Olive oil
Salt and freshly ground black pepper
2 tablespoons (28 grams) unsalted butter
1 garlic clove, crushed but not peeled
Leaves from 3 thyme sprigs
Juice of ½ lemon

## The mushrooms

It's best to clean mushrooms with a brush, a damp cloth, and/or a small pointed knife, but if they are very dirty, remove as much dirt as possible with the knife, then dip them very briefly in cold water, drain them immediately, and dry with a paper towel or a cloth. (Mushrooms should never soak in water for more than 30 seconds.) Cut bigger mushrooms lengthwise in half; leave smaller ones whole.

## The yogurt-hazelnut sauce

Put the yogurt, hazelnuts, Parmesan, herb leaves, a drizzle of hazelnut oil, and a pinch of salt in a blender and mix until creamy. If the sauce is too thick, add a drop or two of water. Adjust the salt if necessary and refrigerate. (The sauce can be refrigerated for up to 2 days.) Use extra as a delicious dip for raw vegetables, or serve it with fried chicken.

## The garnish

Toast the hazelnuts with a pinch of salt in a small dry skillet until they are golden brown. Let them cool, then coarsely crush them.

Separate the grapes from the stems. With a vegetable peeler, cut thin shavings from the cheese. Remove the tarragon leaves from the stems.

## Finishing touches

Heat a drizzle of olive oil in a very large skillet over medium-high heat. When the oil starts to smoke, throw in the mushrooms and sauté them for 8 to 12 minutes, or until tender (timing will depend on the type of mushrooms). Season with salt and pepper, then add the butter, garlic, and thyme. When the butter is foaming, add the grapes and tarragon leaves, stir gently, and add the lemon juice. Taste and adjust the seasonings if needed.

Arrange the mushrooms on four plates, scatter the crushed hazelnuts and cheese shavings over them, and drizzle with some of the sauce.

*Sautéed Wild Mushrooms*
with Grapes and **Aged Mimolette**

# *Butternut Squash* **Risotto** with **Amaretti**

4 servings / Wine pairing: Graves white (Sauvignon/Sémillon); Domaine de Chevalier

I love the balance of salty and sweet in this risotto, with the sweetness of the creamy roasted squash puree and crunchy amaretti cookies offset by the grated and shaved Parmesan.

You could use store-bought chicken broth, but the taste of homemade chicken broth is incomparable and well worth the effort. Ideally, you should prepare the broth a day ahead. I like to use nonclassic flavors, such as ginger and lemongrass, in this broth, which give it freshness and make a wonderful counterpoint to the squash and amaretti. You will have extra broth; freeze the rest for another dish.

**FOR THE CHICKEN BROTH**
1 carrot
1 leek
1 celery stalk
1 onion
½ fennel bulb
1 lemongrass stalk
1 garlic clove
⅔ ounce (20 grams) fresh ginger
3 thyme sprigs
4 white peppercorns
1 teaspoon fennel seeds
2 pounds (1 kg.) chicken bones and/or
    wings from free-range chickens

**FOR THE BUTTERNUT SQUASH PUREE**
½ small butternut squash
1 tablespoon olive oil
1 garlic clove, crushed
Salt
Piment d'Espelette
Juice of ½ lemon, or to taste

**FOR THE GARNISH**
4 ounces (100 grams) Brussels sprouts
About 6 sage sprigs
Olive oil
Salt
Sherry vinegar
8 amaretti cookies
Parmesan shavings

**FOR THE RISOTTO**
5 cups (1.25 liters) chicken broth,
    or as needed
2 shallots
4 tablespoons (56 grams) unsalted
    butter
Olive oil
1 bay leaf
Salt
1¾ cups (300 grams) carnaroli
    or arborio rice
½ cup (100 ml.) dry white wine
Generous ¼ cup (70 grams)
    freshly grated Parmesan
Juice of ½ lemon, or to taste
Piment d'Espelette

## The chicken broth

Chop the carrot, leek, celery, onion, and fennel into 1-inch pieces.

Combine all the vegetables, the lemongrass, garlic, ginger, thyme sprigs, peppercorns, and fennel seeds in a large pot, add the chicken bones, cover with water, and bring to a boil. Lower the heat and simmer for about 1½ hours, skimming off the foam regularly. Turn off the heat and let the broth infuse for another 30 minutes as it cools.

Strain the broth and refrigerate (it will keep for up to 3 days). Remove any hardened fat before using.

## The butternut squash

Preheat the oven to 350°F.

With a sharp spoon, remove the seeds and strings from the squash; reserve about 1 tablespoon of the seeds. Peel the squash, dice into ¾-inch pieces, and place in a large bowl. Toss with the olive oil, crushed garlic, and salt and piment d'Espelette to taste. Spread on a baking sheet and roast for about 20 minutes: the squash is done when it mashes easily under your fingers.

Meanwhile, toss the reserved squash seeds with a pinch of salt, spread on a small baking sheet, and toast in

the oven for 10 to 15 minutes, stirring every 5 minutes. Set aside.

Transfer the squash to a blender, add the lemon juice, and puree. Add a little water if necessary to obtain a smooth puree. Taste and adjust the seasoning. Set aside.

## The garnish

With a small knife, cut the outer leaves from the Brussels sprouts, keeping only the pretty ones. Save the "hearts" for another use.

Remove the sage leaves from the stems. Fry them in a small quantity of olive oil in a small skillet over medium-low heat, making sure they don't burn. The sage leaves are ready when they become translucent. Drain on paper towels. Save the sage-infused oil for garnish.

## The risotto

Heat the 5 cups chicken broth in a saucepan and keep it warm over low heat. Peel and dice the shallots.

Melt 2 tablespoons of the butter with a dash of olive oil in a medium pot over medium heat. Add the shallots, bay leaf, and a pinch of salt and cook until the shallots are softened, about 3 minutes; avoid browning them. Reduce the heat to medium-low, add the rice, stirring so each grain is coated with fat, and cook the rice for 3 to 5 minutes to toast it. Turn

up the heat slightly, deglaze the pan with the white wine, stirring, and cook until the wine has evaporated. Add a small ladleful of broth, stir, and cook, stirring until the liquid is absorbed by the rice. Continue cooking, stirring and adding more broth as necessary, until the rice is al dente and the risotto is creamy, about 17 minutes.

## Finishing touches

Add ¼ cup of the butternut squash puree to the risotto and mix well (reserve the remaining puree for another use). Turn off the heat and let the risotto rest for 5 minutes (don't forget to remove the bay leaf).

Meanwhile, briefly sauté the leaves from the Brussels sprouts in a bit of olive oil with a pinch of salt. Add a dash of sherry vinegar, and drain on paper towels.

Add the remaining 2 tablespoons butter, the grated Parmesan, and the lemon juice to the risotto and give a good stir. If it is too thick, add a bit more chicken broth to loosen it. Taste and season with salt and piment d'Espelette.

Divide the risotto among 4 bowls. Top with the Brussels sprout leaves, fried sage, and toasted squash seeds. Crumble the amaretti over the top, finish with the Parmesan shavings and a drizzle of sage-infused oil, and serve immediately.

*Butternut Squash*
**Risotto** with **Amaretti**

# Sea Scallops with *Parsnip Puree*, Parsnip Chips, and Sorrel

4 servings / Wine pairing: Late-harvest German Riesling (Spätlese); Egon Müller

The sweetness of scallops and parsnips is wonderfully balanced by the acidity of sorrel, the tart apple, and the radish pickles. I love the sourness and soft crunch of these pickles, which bring a new dimension to myriad dishes.

**FOR THE RADISH PICKLES**
1 large bunch radishes (about 15)
1¼ cups (300 ml.) rice vinegar or white wine vinegar
Scant ½ cup (100 ml.) water
½ cup (100 grams) granulated sugar
2 pinches fine sea salt

12 fresh plump sea scallops

**FOR THE PARSNIP PUREE AND CHIPS**
3 parsnips
1 cup (250 ml.) whole milk
Fine sea salt
About 3 cups (750 ml.) vegetable oil, for deep-frying

**FOR THE GARNISH**
About 12 sorrel leaves
1 Granny Smith apple
Juice of ½ lemon

Olive oil
2 tablespoons (28 grams) unsalted butter
1 thyme sprig
1 garlic clove, crushed
Fleur de sel
Piment d'Espelette

## The radish pickles

Trim the radishes and reserve 4 whole radishes for garnish. Cut the others into quarters and place in a bowl.

Combine the rice vinegar, water, sugar, and salt in a small nonreactive saucepan and bring to a boil, stirring to dissolve the sugar and salt. Pour over the quartered radishes and let cool to room temperature, then refrigerate. (The radishes will keep for several days.)

## The scallops

Meanwhile, rinse the scallops under cold water and pat dry with paper towels. Put them on a plate, arranging them tightly together so they stay firm. Refrigerate.

## The parsnip puree

Peel the parsnips. Set 1 aside for the chips. Slice the other 2 into 1-inch chunks; cut the thicker chunks lengthwise in half. Put in a small saucepan and pour in the milk. Bring to a boil (be careful that it doesn't boil over), then lower the heat and simmer until the parsnips mash easily under a spoon, 15 to 18 minutes.

Using a slotted spoon, transfer the parsnips to a blender. Add half the milk and puree, adding more of the milk if necessary, then return to the saucepan and season with salt to taste. Set aside.

## The parsnip chips

With a vegetable peeler, slice the reserved parsnip into long, thin strips.

Heat the vegetable oil to 350°F in a medium deep saucepan. Fry the parsnip strips, in batches, to a golden color, 30 seconds to 1 minute. Drain on paper towels and immediately sprinkle with salt.

## The garnish

Remove the center stems from the sorrel (fold the leaves in half and strip out the stems).

With a mandoline, cut the apple into thin slices (discard the center slices with the core) and toss with the lemon juice to prevent them from browning. Set aside.

Thinly slice the reserved radishes.

## The scallops

Heat a large skillet over high heat. Generously coat the scallops with olive oil and place them in the (very hot) pan; don't add salt yet—it will make them tough. Cook for 1 minute on the first side, then add the butter, thyme, and crushed garlic. Once the butter is foaming, turn the scallops over, sprinkle with fleur de sel and piment d'Espelette, and baste with the butter for 30 seconds, or until just cooked through. Drain briefly on paper towels.

Meanwhile, gently reheat the parsnip puree.

## To serve

Spoon the parsnip puree into four shallow bowls. Lay a nest of parsnip chips on each plate, top with 3 scallops, and harmoniously arrange some of the radish pickles, sorrel leaves, apple slices, and sliced radishes in each bowl.

**Sea Scallops** with *Parsnip Puree,* **Parsnip Chips,** and Sorrel

# **Pork** Braised in Milk
## with *Marinated Fennel*

4 servings / Wine pairing: Burgundy white (Viognier); Condrieu Georges Vernay

Pork shoulder is one of my favorite cuts: it is full of collagen, which will soften and melt during the long slow cooking and make the meat very tender and tasty. This is an Italian-inspired dish, using techniques I learned at The River Café in London. The milk proteins also help soften the pork, and then the milky curds are served with the meat.

**FOR THE PORK**
One 2-pound (1-kg.) boneless pork
   shoulder roast
Salt and freshly ground black pepper
About 6 sage sprigs
1 lemon
2 salt-packed anchovies (or substitute
   4 oil-packed anchovy fillets)

Grapeseed oil
1 tablespoon (14 grams) unsalted butter
½ garlic clove, crushed
About 5 cups (1.25 liters) whole milk

**FOR THE MARINATED FENNEL**
6 baby or 3 medium fennel bulbs
1 small chile pepper

¼ bunch dill
Salt
1½ teaspoons fennel seeds
Grated zest and juice of 1 lemon
Olive oil
Coarse sea salt

## The pork

Preheat the oven to 350°F.

Season the pork shoulder with salt and pepper. Set aside.

Tie the sage sprigs together with kitchen string. With a vegetable peeler, remove the zest from the lemon in strips, making sure to avoid the bitter white pith. If using salt-packed anchovies, rinse under cold water and remove the 2 fillets from each one.

Heat a large Dutch oven over medium-high heat. Add a drizzle of grapeseed oil and then add the pork, fat side down. Brown the meat on all sides, 3 to 4 minutes per side, then transfer it to a plate.

Pour off the fat from the pot, put it back over medium heat, add the butter, and deglaze the pot with a wooden spoon, scraping up all the meaty browned bits. When the butter starts to foam, add the sage, garlic, anchovies, and lemon zest and cook over low heat, stirring, until the anchovies dissolve.

Add the pork shoulder and pour in enough milk to come about halfway up the sides of the meat. Bring to a simmer, then cover tightly with the lid, put the pot in the oven, and cook for 2½ to 3 hours, turning the meat every 30 minutes and adding milk as needed, until the pork is tender and separates easily and the milk has reduced and curdled. If the pork is cooked but the milk has not reduced and curdled, remove the meat from the pot, place the pot over medium heat, and cook until the milk has reduced. Then return the pork to the pot and cover to keep warm.

## The marinated fennel

Meanwhile, bring a medium pot of water to a boil.

Trim the fennel bulbs, halve lengthwise, and cut each half into 3 wedges.

Cut the chile pepper lengthwise in half, remove the seeds, and finely mince the pepper. Chop the dill.

Generously salt the boiling water, throw in the fennel seeds, and add the fennel wedges. Cook for 6 to 9 minutes; the fennel should be tender but still have a slight crunch. Drain the fennel pieces and put in a baking dish in a single layer. Let cool for a few minutes, then add the chile pepper, chopped dill, and lemon zest. Add lemon juice to taste, drizzle with olive oil, and toss gently with your hands. Season with coarse salt to taste.

## To serve

With a large spoon, separate the pork into chunks and divide among four plates. Top each with a spoonful of milk curds and arrange the marinated fennel wedges alongside. The pork is best served just slightly warm.

**Pork** Braised in Milk
with *Marinated Fennel*

# Beef Cheeks **with Roasted Beets, Watercress,** *and Grated Horseradish*

**4 servings / Wine pairing: Cahors red (Malbec); Mas del Périé**

This is comfort food with a twist, where the sweetness of the beets is lightened by the raspberry vinaigrette, and the beef cheeks are "peppered" with watercress and horseradish. Beef cheeks are a tough, lean cut, with a lot of collagen, and need to cook very slowly. Properly cooked, they turn soft and almost caramelized, a bit like pulled pork. You'll need to order them ahead from a specialty butcher; or see Sources, page 137. Plan ahead, as cooking the meat can take up to 4 hours.

Roasting the beets covered on a bed of salt steams them while intensifying the flavors. If you can find tiny new beets at the farmers' market, even better—adjust the cooking time as necessary, and then leave them whole.

**FOR THE BEEF CHEEKS**
2 large beef cheeks (2 to 2½ pounds/
   1 kg. total), trimmed of excess fat
Salt and freshly ground black pepper
1 carrot
1 onion
1 celery stalk
½ leek
⅓ ounce (10 grams) fresh ginger
Grapeseed oil or sunflower oil
1 tablespoon coriander seeds
1 tablespoon fennel seeds
½ star anise

½ cinnamon stick
1 lemongrass stalk
Peel of ½ orange
1 tablespoon tomato paste
½ bottle (1½ cups/375 ml.) dry red wine
1 bouquet garni (a few thyme and
   parsley sprigs and a bay leaf, tied
   together with kitchen string)

**FOR THE BEETS**
12 to 16 baby beets
   (about 1½ pounds/700 grams)
½ cup coarse sea salt

¾ cup plus 2 tablespoons (200 ml.)
   beet juice

Red wine vinegar
Salt
3 tablespoons fine kasha (roasted
   buckwheat)
Raspberry vinegar
1 bunch chives, finely chopped
¾ ounce (20 grams) fresh horseradish,
   grated
A handful of watercress leaves

## The beef cheeks

Preheat the oven to 350°F.

Cut the beef cheeks in half. Season lightly with salt and pepper.

Peel the carrot. Cut the carrot, onion, celery, and leek into 1-inch pieces. Chop the ginger.

Heat a Dutch oven over medium-high heat. Add a drizzle of grapeseed oil and brown the meat on all sides, 6 to 8 minutes per side, then remove it from the pot.

Add the vegetables to the pot and cook for about 5 minutes, until beginning to soften. Add all the spices, the lemongrass,

ginger, orange peel, and tomato paste and cook, stirring, for 5 minutes. Add the red wine and bring to a simmer.

Put the meat back in the pot, along with the bouquet garni, and add water to cover the meat almost entirely. Bring to a boil, then cover tightly, put the pot in the oven, and braise for 3 to 3½ hours, checking the level of liquid every 30 minutes and adding boiling water if necessary, until the meat is very tender and almost melts in your mouth; halfway through cooking, turn the cheeks over.

## The beets

Meanwhile, wash the beets under cold water, using a brush if necessary. Spread the coarse salt in a baking dish and

lay the beets on top. Cover tightly with two layers of foil and bake for 45 minutes to 1 hour, depending on the size of the beets, until tender: the tip of a knife should go through a beet without any resistance. Let the beets stand until cool enough to be handled.

With an old cloth (beet stains are hard to remove) or paper towels, rub off the beets' skin; it should come off easily. Dice or quarter the beets into bite-sized pieces. Set aside.

Bring the beet juice to a boil in a small saucepan and boil it to reduce by half. Set aside.

## Finishing touches

When the beef is cooked, transfer it to a plate. Strain the braising liquid into a small pot, bring to a boil, and reduce it until slightly thickened. Add a dash of red wine vinegar and adjust the salt. Return the beef cheeks to the sauce and reheat.

Meanwhile, warm the beets in the beet juice. Remove from the heat, add the buckwheat, cover, and let it swell for about 5 minutes. Add a dash of raspberry vinegar and the chives, taste, and adjust the salt if necessary.

Divide the beets among four shallow bowls. Add a piece of beef cheek to each and cover with the sauce. Garnish each plate with some grated horseradish and a few sprigs of watercress. Serve immediately.

Beef Cheeks **with Roasted Beets, Watercress,** *and Grated Horseradish*

# **Pear,** Turnip, *and* **Pecorino Pepato Salad**

**4 servings / Wine pairing: Vouvray (Chenin Blanc); Sébastien Brunet**

Quick to prepare and delicious, this versatile little salad can be served as a starter, a light lunch, or a cheese course/dessert. The shaved pecorino pepato, a delicious hard Italian cheese studded with black peppercorns, is my way of seasoning the salad—it adds sharpness, salt, and pepper all at once. Make sure you use baby turnips, which can be eaten raw.

**4 juicy pears, such as Red Bartlett or Comice**

**4 baby turnips (the size of a golf ball or smaller)**

**A handful of baby dandelion greens**
**Fleur de sel**
**Extra virgin olive oil**
**Juice of ½ lemon**

**3½ ounces (100 grams) pecorino pepato cheese**

Quarter and core the pears. With a mandoline, slice the turnips very thin. Separate the dandelion leaves.

Put the pear wedges, turnip slices, and dandelion leaves in a large bowl and gently toss with a pinch of fleur de sel, 2 tablespoons olive oil, and the lemon juice.

Arrange the salad on four plates. Using a vegetable peeler, thinly shave the pecorino pepato over the salads. Finish with a drizzle of olive oil.

# *Poached Quinces* with Chestnut Cream
# **and Chocolate Shavings**

4 servings / Wine pairing: Calvados; Adrien Camus (35-year-old)

This is a dessert for the first chilly nights by the fire. Chocolate, chestnuts,
and quince are soothing flavors that marry well.

**FOR THE POACHED QUINCES**
½ vanilla bean
¾ cup (150 grams) granulated sugar
⅔ cup (150 ml.) dry white wine
⅔ cup (150 ml.) water
Zest of ½ orange, removed in strips with
    a vegetable peeler

Zest of ½ lemon, removed in strips
    with a vegetable peeler
2 small quinces

**FOR THE CHESTNUT CREAM**
⅓ cup (75 ml.) very cold heavy cream
2 tablespoons (50 grams)
    sweet chestnut puree
About 1 teaspoon rum (optional)

**FOR THE GARNISH**
4 candied chestnuts
Grated zest of ½ orange
¾ ounce (20 grams)
    70% bittersweet chocolate

## The poached quinces

With a small knife, split the vanilla bean and scrape out the seeds; reserve the bean and seeds.

Combine the sugar, white wine, water, orange and lemon zest, and vanilla bean and seeds in a medium nonreactive saucepan and bring to a boil, stirring to dissolve the sugar. Remove from the heat and let the liquid steep while you prepare the quinces.

Cut off the tops and bottoms of the quinces, then cut each one into 6 uniform wedges so they will cook evenly. Remove the skin by holding each wedge in one hand and cutting the skin away in a curved motion with a sharp paring knife. Remove the seeds with a curved cut.

Submerge the quince wedges in the poaching syrup, bring to a simmer, and simmer, turning the wedges occasionally, for 20 to 30 minutes, depending on the ripeness of the fruit. The quinces should be tender but still have a slight crunch. Remove from the heat and let cool to lukewarm in the poaching syrup.

## The chestnut cream

Meanwhile, with an electric mixer, whip the cream just until it holds firm peaks. Put the chestnut puree in a small bowl and stir in a little of the cream, then gently fold in the remaining cream. Add the rum if desired.

## To serve

Place a large quenelle or a generous spoonful of chestnut cream in each of four shallow bowls. Arrange 3 lukewarm quince wedges around each one and coat with the syrup. Garnish each serving with a candied chestnut and some orange zest, and grate the chocolate over the top.

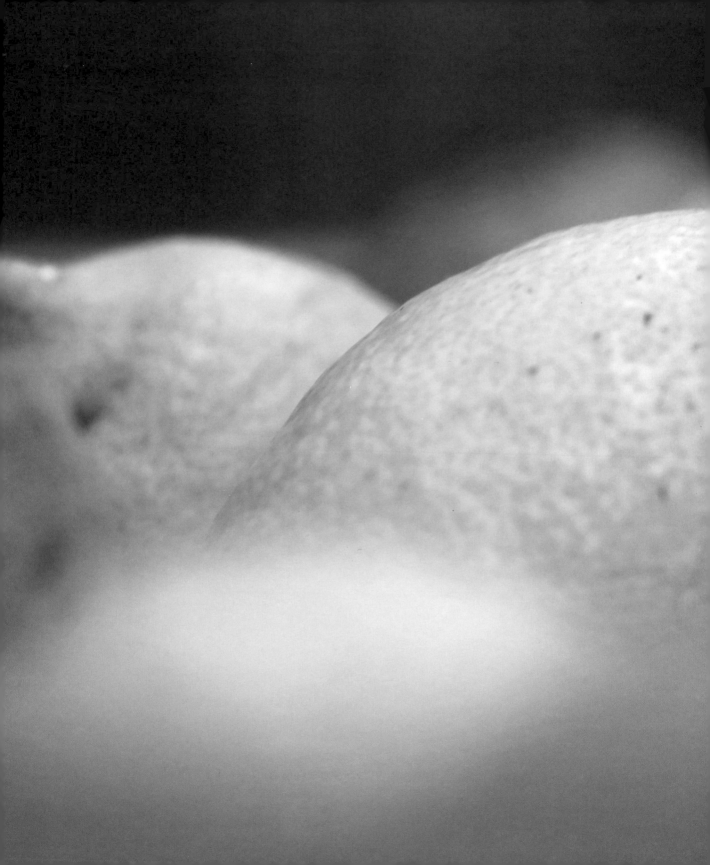

# winter

# **Salad of** *Bitter Greens*
## with Speck **and Clementine**

**4 servings / Wine pairing: Sancerre (Sauvignon Blanc); Jean-Dominique Vacheron**

When fresh greens are scarce in the winter, this is a lovely salad alternative, which combines sweet, salty, smoky, and bitter flavors, brightened by the refreshing taste of mint. You can use tangerines instead of clementines and bresaola instead of speck, as long as you keep the four flavors in balance.

4 clementines
12 mint leaves
A big handful of bitter greens, such
    as radicchio, dandelion, arugula,
    purslane, and/or watercress

Juice of ½ lemon, or to taste
Olive oil
Fleur de sel
Freshly ground black pepper
8 thin slices speck

Parmesan shavings
Balsamic vinegar

Peel the clementines and cut them into ¼-inch-thick wheels. Put them in a bowl and add the mint and greens. Season with the lemon juice, a drizzle of olive oil, a pinch of fleur de sel, and pepper, and toss gently with your hands. Taste and adjust the seasoning (be careful not to add too much salt, as the speck and Parmesan are salty).

Arrange the salad and speck slices on four plates and add some Parmesan shavings, a drizzle of olive oil, and a drizzle of balsamic vinegar to each one. Serve.

# Blood Sausage with Burrata
## and *Apple Chutney*

4 servings / Wine pairing: New Zealand Sauvignon Blanc; Shaw & Smith

This delicious dish is all about contrasts: the black blood sausage versus the pure white burrata, rustic meaty flavors versus the delicate creaminess of the cheese. I like *boudin* from the Basque country, which has very little fat. For this recipe, use a young very green olive oil, which complements the subtle taste of the burrata.

I fell in love with chutneys when I was working in England, and I make them all the time. The apple chutney will keep in the refrigerator for several months. It can also be served with foie gras, cheese, or charcuterie.

**FOR THE APPLE CHUTNEY**
1 small onion
Juice of ½ lemon
1 pound (450 grams) tart apples, such as Pippin or Granny Smith
6 tablespoons (95 ml.) white wine vinegar
Scant 3 tablespoons (70 grams) granulated sugar

Scant 3 tablespoons (70 grams) brown sugar
½ teaspoon mustard seeds
¼ cinnamon stick
2 tablespoons (50 grams) small raisins

About 14 ounces (600 grams) blood sausage
2 burratas (about 8 ounces/225 grams each), halved

Fleur de sel
Freshly ground black pepper
Extra virgin olive oil (see the headnote)
A few leaves of bitter greens, such as endive, radicchio, or dandelion
½ Granny Smith apple, cut into ⅓-inch cubes
½ lemon

## The apple chutney

Peel and finely chop the onion.

Fill a medium bowl with water and add the lemon juice. Peel, halve, and core the apples, then cut into ½-inch cubes and immediately put them in the lemon water so they don't oxidize and turn brown.

Combine the chopped onion, vinegar, sugars, mustard seeds, and cinnamon in a medium nonreactive saucepan and bring to a boil, stirring to dissolve the sugar, then lower the heat and simmer until the liquid has reduced to a thin syrup, about 10 minutes.

Add the apples and raisins to the syrup and cook over low heat, stirring regularly so the chutney doesn't stick to the bottom of the pan, until the apples are tender, 18 to 20 minutes.

Pour the hot chutney into a sterilized jar, seal it, and turn it upside down. Let cool to room temperature, then refrigerate.

## The blood sausage

Cut the blood sausage into 1½-inch-long pieces. Heat a nonstick skillet over medium heat. Add the blood sausage and cook for about 5 minutes on each side, until seared and crisp. Drain on paper towels.

## To serve

Place a burrata half on each plate and season with fleur de sel, pepper, and a drizzle of olive oil. Arrange the blood sausage on top of the burrata, then add a spoonful of apple chutney, some bitter green leaves, and a few fresh apple cubes. Finish with a drizzle of olive oil and a squeeze of lemon juice.

**Blood Sausage** with
**Burrata** and *Apple Chutney*

# Mussels with
## *Jerusalem Artichokes* **and Chorizo**

4 servings / Wine pairing: Burgundy red (Pinot Noir); Morgon Jean Foillard

A little stew salad, with Spanish and Portuguese influences in the combination of shellfish and pork. Jerusalem artichokes are one of my favorite root vegetables. They are slightly astringent and go really well with the spicy chorizo and the delicate mussels.

**FOR THE JERUSALEM ARTICHOKES**
1 pound (500 grams) Jerusalem
  artichokes
3 thyme sprigs
2 garlic cloves, crushed but not peeled
Olive oil
Salt and freshly ground black pepper

**FOR THE MUSSELS**
1¼ pounds (680 grams) small mussels
2 shallots
A 1-inch piece of fresh ginger

1 lemongrass stalk
2 teaspoons unsalted butter
Olive oil
1 thyme sprig
Zest of 1 lemon, removed in strips
  with a vegetable peeler
½ star anise
¼ teaspoon fennel seeds
¼ teaspoon coriander seeds
1 teaspoon white peppercorns
Scant 1 cup (200 ml.) dry white wine

A handful of flat-leaf parsley, dill,
  and tarragon leaves
3½ ounces (100 grams) Spanish chorizo
Olive oil
3 tablespoons (42 grams) unsalted
  butter
Juice of 1 lemon, or to taste
Salt
About 3½ ounces (100 grams)
  baby spinach leaves

## The Jerusalem artichokes

Preheat the oven to 350°F.

Scrub the Jerusalem artichokes with a brush under cold running water; drain well. Combine the artichokes, thyme sprigs, crushed garlic, and a drizzle of olive oil in a bowl, season with salt and pepper, and toss well.

Spread the Jerusalem artichokes on a baking sheet and roast, turning once or twice, for 28 to 30 minutes: they should hold their shape but be soft to the touch. Let them cool, then cut lengthwise in half. Set aside.

## The mussels

Scrub and debeard the mussels. Peel and mince the shallots. Peel and finely chop the ginger. Finely chop the lemongrass.

Melt the butter with a drizzle of oil in a large pot over medium heat. Add the shallots, ginger, lemongrass, thyme, lemon zest, star anise, fennel and coriander seeds, and peppercorns and cook over low heat until the shallots soften, about 5 minutes. Add the white wine and bring to a simmer over medium-high heat. Add the mussels, cover, and cook until they open, 3 to 5 minutes. Remove them with a slotted spoon (reserve the cooking liquid). Shell the mussels and refrigerate. Strain the cooking liquid and set aside.

## Finishing touches

Chop the herbs. Dice the chorizo into ¼-inch cubes.

Heat a splash of olive oil over medium-high heat in a skillet large enough to hold the Jerusalem artichokes in one layer. When the oil is hot, lay the artichokes cut side down in the pan and cook until golden brown on the bottom, about 3 minutes. Add the chorizo, turn the Jerusalem artichokes, and cook for another minute. Deglaze the pan with the mussel cooking liquid, stirring well, then add the butter, bring to a boil, and boil until the sauce is slightly reduced. Add the chopped herbs, mussels, and a splash of lemon juice and heat through, then taste and add salt and more lemon juice if needed.

Remove from the heat, add the spinach leaves, and toss well, then serve immediately.

# **Roast Pork,** Red Beet Broth, and Pickled Mustard Seeds

4 to 6 servings / Wine pairing: Burgundy red (Pinot Noir); Joseph Roty

This is a simple peasant dish, wonderfully comforting on cold winter nights. In France, pork loin roasts are generally sold with a thicker layer of fat than those in the United States, as you will see in the photo on page 118 (top left); I've also made this with pork belly, which is a little fattier. The acidity of the beet broth and pickled mustard balance the richness of the meat. The extra pickled mustard seeds will keep for weeks; serve alongside a charcuterie platter or use as a condiment in sandwiches.

**FOR THE PICKLED MUSTARD SEEDS**
Scant 4 ounces (1¼ cups/125 grams) mustard seeds
¾ cup (175 ml.) rice vinegar
¾ cup (175 ml.) water
6 tablespoons (62 grams) granulated sugar
1 teaspoon salt

**FOR THE BEET BROTH**
2 cups (500 ml.) beet juice
7 tablespoons (100 ml.) apple juice
4 teaspoons (20 grams) grated fresh ginger

**FOR THE GARNISH**
¼ cup (100 grams) green lentils (lentilles du Puy)
1 bouquet garni (a few thyme and parsley sprigs and a bay leaf, tied together with kitchen string)
Olive oil
Salt
3 carrots, preferably 1 each yellow, purple, and orange

**FOR THE ROAST PORK**
Salt
1 boneless pork loin roast, about 2 pounds (1 kg.)

Olive oil (if the pork has very little fat)
3 tablespoons (42 grams) unsalted butter
3 thyme sprigs
3 rosemary sprigs
2 garlic cloves, crushed

Cider vinegar
Raspberry vinegar
Salt and freshly ground black pepper
1 bunch chives, chopped
Fleur de sel
Crushed black pepper

## The pickled mustard seeds

Combine the mustard seeds, vinegar, water, sugar, and salt in a medium heavy nonreactive saucepan and bring to a boil, stirring to dissolve the sugar and salt, then lower the heat and simmer for 45 minutes, or until the mustard seeds swell and soften slightly; add more water if necessary.

Let cool, then refrigerate. (The mustard seeds will keep for up to 2 months.)

## The beet broth

Combine both the juices and the ginger in a medium saucepan and bring to a boil, then reduce the heat and simmer until reduced by half, removing the foam regularly. Strain and refrigerate.

## The garnish

Put the lentils in a medium saucepan, cover with water by 2 inches, and add the bouquet garni and a drizzle of olive oil. Bring to a simmer and simmer gently until tender, 25 to 30 minutes. Season the lentils with salt and set aside.

Meanwhile, peel the carrots and cut them into ½-inch cubes. Add them to a saucepan of boiling salted water and cook until tender, about 8 minutes. Drain and set aside.

## The roast pork

Preheat the oven to 350°F.

Salt the pork loin generously. Heat a large ovenproof skillet over medium-high heat. Unless the pork has a thick layer of fat, add a splash of olive oil to the pan and heat it. Add the

pork, fat side down, and cook until browned and crisp, about 6 minutes. Turn the pork and brown on the second side, about 4 minutes, then brown the remaining 2 sides. Transfer the pan to the oven and roast for 18 to 20 minutes, or until the internal temperature reaches 135°F on an instant-read thermometer.

Take the pan out of the oven and spoon off the fat. Add the butter, herbs, and garlic cloves and heat over high heat until the butter foams, then baste the meat, turning once, for about 2 minutes on each side. Transfer to a rack and let rest for 15 minutes, then cut into thick slices.

## Finishing touches

Meanwhile, pour the beet broth into a saucepan and bring it to a boil. Add the carrots and heat over low heat for about 5 minutes. Drain the lentils, remove the bouquet garni, add the lentils to the broth, and heat through. Remove from the heat and season the broth with a dash of cider vinegar, another dash of raspberry vinegar, and salt and pepper to taste. Add the chopped chives.

Divide the broth and vegetables among shallow bowls, then top each with a slice of pork. Spoon over some pickled mustard seeds and finish with a pinch each of fleur de sel and crushed pepper.

**Roast Pork,** Red Beet Broth,
and Pickled Mustard Seeds

# Panfried Duck Breast,
## *Orange-Infused Celeriac,* and **Candied Kumquats**

4 servings / Wine pairing: Sardinian red (Grenache); Gianfranco Manca

This is my take on duck à l'orange. Although very different from the classic dish, it uses similar flavor combinations. Celeriac is one of my favorite vegetables, especially with a splash of lemon. During the winter, I use a lot of citrus fruit to add sparkle to a dish. The candied kumquats provide a fragrant combination of acidity and sweetness.

Magrets are the big, meaty breasts of moulard ducks (which are raised for foie gras); see Sources, page 137. Or, if necessary, substitute 4 smaller breasts from Pekin (Long Island) or Muscovy ducks and adjust the cooking time accordingly.

**FOR THE CANDIED KUMQUATS**
7 ounces (200 grams) kumquats
¾ cup (120 grams) granulated sugar
Scant ½ teaspoon coarse sea salt
1 star anise
Juice of 1 lemon

**FOR THE BRAISED AND PUREED CELERIAC**
1 celeriac
1½ cups (350 ml.) orange juice
2 teaspoons unsalted butter
1 thyme sprig

2 cups (500 ml.) whole milk, or as needed
1 bay leaf
Salt
Juice of 1 lemon, or to taste

**FOR THE PORT SAUCE**
2 cups (500 ml.) port
¼ teaspoon fennel seeds
¼ teaspoon coriander seeds
Dash of sherry vinegar

**FOR THE DUCK BREASTS**
2 magrets (Moulard duck breasts), about 1 pound (480 grams) each

Salt
1 teaspoon unsalted butter
1 garlic clove, crushed
1 thyme sprig
1 rosemary sprig
Freshly ground black pepper

**TO FINISH**
Fleur de sel
Freshly ground black pepper
A few dill sprigs

## The candied kumquats

Put the kumquats in a medium heavy nonreactive saucepan, cover with cold water, and bring to a boil, then drain in a colander and cool under cold water. (This will help remove some bitterness from the fruit.)

Halve the kumquats lengthwise and remove the seeds. Put them back in the pan and add the sugar, salt, star anise, and water just to cover. Bring to a simmer and simmer very gently for about 45 minutes, adding a little water if needed to keep the kumquats covered, until the peel is very tender. Remove from the heat and remove the star anise.

Using a slotted spoon, transfer the kumquats to a blender, preferably a heavy-duty one. Add some of the poaching syrup and puree, adding more poaching syrup as necessary. Mix in the lemon juice. Set aside.

## The braised celeriac

Trim the celeriac and peel it. Cut a 1-inch-thick slice from the center of the celeriac and cut it into 6 wedges (see the photo on page 123). Reserve the remaining celeriac for the puree.

Put the celeriac wedges in a small nonreactive saucepan and add the orange juice, butter, and thyme. Bring just to a simmer and simmer gently for 20 to 25 minutes. Check a wedge with a knife: if the knife goes in effortlessly, it's done. Set aside in the cooking liquid.

## The celeriac puree

Cut the remaining celeriac into ½-inch cubes. Put in a medium saucepan and add enough milk to cover, then add the bay leaf and a pinch of salt. Bring to a simmer and simmer gently until the celeriac is very tender, 25 to 30 minutes.

Using a slotted spoon, transfer the celeriac to a blender and puree, adding a little bit of the cooking liquid if needed. Season to taste with salt and a squeeze of lemon juice. Set aside.

## The port sauce

Meanwhile, combine the port and seeds in a medium saucepan, bring to a boil, and boil until reduced to a syrupy consistency, 20 to 25 minutes. Season with a dash of sherry vinegar, strain into a small saucepan, and set aside.

## The duck breasts

Trim the duck breasts, removing the excess fat and the strip of sinew from each one. Score the skin and fat with the tip of a sharp knife in a crisscross design, making sure not to pierce the meat. (This will help the fat to render.) Season with salt only on the skin side.

Heat a large skillet over high heat until very hot, then add the breasts skin side down and cook over low heat, carefully removing the melted fat along the way, until the skin is browned and crispy, 8 to 10 minutes. Add the butter, garlic, and herbs and turn up the heat so the butter foams. Season the flesh side with salt and pepper, then turn the breasts over. Cook, basting with the butter and fat, for about 30 seconds for very rare, or about 2 minutes for just rare. Transfer to a rack and let rest for 15 minutes in a warm spot.

## Finishing touches

While the duck rests, reheat the celeriac puree, braised celeriac, and sauce. Once the braised celeriac is warm, remove it from the pan and keep warm, then boil the cooking liquid to reduce it slightly.

Spoon some celeriac puree onto each plate in a swirl. Add a spoonful of candied kumquat puree and a wedge of braised celeriac, topped with some of the reduced cooking liquid.

Slice the duck breasts and arrange them on the plates. Season each with a pinch of fleur de sel and pepper. Finish with the sauce and the dill sprigs.

**Panfried Duck Breast,**
*Orange-Infused Celeriac,*
and **Candied Kumquats**

# Chocolate and Passion Fruit **Pots de Crème** with **Lychees** and Candied Ginger

**4 servings / Wine pairing: Banyuls ambré (Grenache); Philippe Gard Coume del Mas**

In the winter, it's difficult to find any local fruit other than apples and pears in Paris, so I often indulge in exotic flavors, such as mango, pineapple, and passion fruit. Serve the extra passion fruit caramel over ice cream or other desserts.

**FOR THE PASSION FRUIT CARAMEL**
½ cup (100 grams) granulated sugar
2 tablespoons water
Generous 2 tablespoons heavy cream
Generous 2 tablespoons unsweetened
   passion fruit juice
Scant 2 tablespoons (25 grams)
   salted butter

**FOR THE CANDIED GINGER**
3½ ounces (100 grams) fresh ginger
1¼ cups (300 ml.) water
Scant ½ cup (110 ml.) honey
Juice of 1 lemon, or to taste

**FOR THE CHOCOLATE
POTS DE CRÈME**
4½ ounces (125 grams)
   65% bittersweet chocolate
¾ cup plus 1 tablespoon (200 ml.)
   heavy cream
½ cup (125 ml.) whole milk
¼ cup (50 grams) granulated sugar
3 large egg yolks, beaten

12 lychees

## The passion fruit caramel

Combine the sugar with the water in a small heavy nonreactive saucepan and heat over medium heat, stirring just until the sugar dissolves, then cook, swirling the pan for even cooking, until you have a golden brown caramel. Remove from the heat and add the cream and passion fruit juice (be careful—the hot caramel will spatter) and whisk vigorously. Gradually add the butter, whisking until completely incorporated. Let cool, then refrigerate for at least 2 hours.

## The candied ginger

Meanwhile, peel the ginger and dice it into ⅛-inch cubes.

Bring the water and honey to a boil in a small heavy saucepan. Add the ginger and cook over low heat, adding a little water if necessary, until the ginger is translucent and the syrup has reduced to a glaze, about 1½ hours. Stir in the lemon juice, and reserve in the refrigerator. (The ginger will keep for several weeks.)

## The chocolate pots de crème

Preheat the oven to 300°F.

Finely chop the chocolate and put it in a medium bowl. Combine the cream, milk, and sugar in a small saucepan and bring to a boil, stirring to dissolve the sugar. Pour over the chocolate and let stand for 30 seconds to melt it, then stir with a heatproof spatula until smooth. Let cool slightly, then add the egg yolks and stir until smooth.

Pour the mixture into four 4-ounce ramekins. Put the ramekins in a baking dish and add enough warm water to come halfway up the sides of the ramekins. Cover the dish with foil and bake for 28 to 30 minutes. The pots are done when they are firm to the touch but still jiggle when gently shaken. Remove from the water bath and let cool. (It is best not to put the pots de crème in the refrigerator: set aside at room temperature and serve the same day.)

## Finishing touches

Peel the lychees and remove the seeds.

Put the pots de crème on serving plates and place a tablespoon of caramel, a teaspoon of candied ginger, and some lychees on each one.

Chocolate and Passion Fruit
**Pots de Crème with Lychees**
and Candied Ginger

# Chamomile **Panna Cotta** and **Citrus Soup**

4 servings / Wine pairing: Sake

This delicate panna cotta is made with less gelatin than many recipes call for, so be sure to allow enough time for it to set. Infusing the cream with chamomile gives it slight notes of hay, and the panna cotta and citrus fruit soup are an exciting combination, both floral and wild, acidic and sweet. I like to serve this dessert with a good sake.

**FOR THE PANNA COTTA**
½ vanilla bean
1¼ cups (350 ml.) heavy cream
3 tablespoons granulated sugar
1 teaspoon crumbled dried chamomile or chamomile tea
1½ sheets (6 grams) gelatin
3 tablespoons (50 ml.) whole milk

**FOR THE CITRUS SOUP**
2 small grapefruits
2 oranges
8 kumquats
2 clementines
½ sheet (2 grams) gelatin
½ cinnamon stick
1 tablespoon honey

Mint leaves

## The panna cotta

With a small knife, split the vanilla bean and scrape out the seeds; reserve the pod and seeds.

Combine the cream, sugar, chamomile, and vanilla seeds and pod in a small nonreactive saucepan and bring to a simmer. Remove from the heat and let infuse for 20 to 30 minutes. Strain through a fine-mesh sieve into a medium bowl.

Meanwhile, put the gelatin in a bowl of cold water and let stand for 10 minutes, or until softened.

Drain the gelatin and squeeze out the excess water. Heat the milk in a small saucepan, just until warm, then add the gelatin and stir to dissolve it. Pour the milk into the infused cream and stir well. Pour into four 4-ounce timbale molds (about 2 inches high and 2 inches wide) or 4-ounce ramekins.

Refrigerate for at least 6 hours, or overnight.

## The citrus soup

Juice 1 of the grapefruits and both oranges; reserve ½ cup of each type of fruit juice.

Quarter the kumquats lengthwise and remove the seeds. Place them in a saucepan, cover with cold water, and bring to a boil. Drain in a colander and rinse under cold water.

With a sharp knife, peel the remaining grapefruit and the clementines, removing the skin and all the bitter white pith. Then cut between the membranes to remove the citrus segments. Combine with the kumquats in a bowl.

Put the gelatin sheet in a bowl of cold water and let stand for 10 minutes, or until softened.

Combine the orange and grapefruit juice, cinnamon, and honey in a small nonreactive saucepan and heat until warm. Drain the gelatin, squeeze out the excess water, and add to the juice, stirring to dissolve it. Let cool to room temperature.

Pour the cooled juice over the fruit segments and refrigerate until chilled.

## To serve

To unmold the panna cottas, briefly place each one in hot water, then invert into a shallow bowl. Pour the citrus soup around (discard the cinnamon stick) and garnish with mint leaves.

# *Brillat-Savarin* **Cheesecake** **with Mango** and Passion Fruit

8 to 10 servings / Wine pairing: Moscato d'Asti (Muscat); Ca d'Gal

I've always loved cheesecake made in the style of a Bavarian cream (that is, gelatin-based rather than baked): it's both rich and airy at the same time. Brillat-Savarin is a wonderful triple-crème cheese from Burgundy, named after the first French gastronome. My cheesemonger once told me that a lot of his Eastern European customers were buying Brillat-Savarin to make cheesecake. So I gave it a try and found that the result was a delicious cheesecake, with a definite French touch.

Note that the cheesecake needs to be refrigerated for at least 4 hours before adding the glaze (and then for at least another 30 minutes before serving).

**FOR THE CHEESECAKE**
6 tablespoons (85 grams) unsalted butter
About 5¼ ounces (150 grams) speculoos, gingersnaps, or cinnamon cookies
1 vanilla bean
3 sheets (12 grams) gelatin
12 ounces (350 grams) Brillat-Savarin cheese (or another triple-crème cheese)

1¾ cups (425 ml.) very cold heavy cream
3 large eggs
¾ cup (140 grams) granulated sugar
Grated zest of 1 lemon
2 tablespoons lemon juice

**FOR THE PASSION FRUIT GLAZE**
2 sheets (8 grams) gelatin
2 passion fruit

1 cup (250 ml.) unsweetened passion fruit juice

**FOR THE MANGO PUREE**
1 ripe mango
Juice of 1 lime, or to taste
3 tablespoons granulated sugar

## The cheesecake

Melt the butter in a small saucepan over low heat.

Crush the cookies into crumbs in a food processor. Add the melted butter and pulse just until incorporated.

Put a bottomless 10-inch square mold on a baking sheet lined with a Silpat or parchment paper; or use a 9-inch springform pan. Pour the crumb mixture into the mold and pat it evenly over the bottom. Refrigerate.

Split the vanilla bean and scrape out the seeds. Put the gelatin in a bowl of cold water and let stand for 10 minutes, or until softened. Carefully remove all the rind from the cheese. Cut the cheese into chunks and set aside to come to room temperature.

With an electric mixer, beat the cream until firm peaks form. Refrigerate.

Combine the eggs and sugar in a large bowl and beat on medium-high speed until pale and tripled in volume. Add the Brillat-Savarin, lemon zest, and vanilla seeds and beat at medium speed until smooth.

Warm the lemon juice in a small saucepan. Drain the gelatin, squeeze out the excess water, and add it to the juice, stirring until dissolved. Add to the cheese mixture and beat at high speed until smooth. Delicately fold in the whipped cream with a rubber spatula.

Pour the mixture into the mold and smooth the top. Refrigerate for at least 4 hours.

## The passion fruit glaze

Put the gelatin in a bowl of cold water to soften. Cut the passion fruit in half and spoon out the seeds; drain the seeds well in a strainer.

Warm ¼ cup of the passion fruit juice in a small saucepan. Drain the gelatin, squeeze out the excess water, add to the warm juice, and stir to dissolve. Add the rest of the juice and the passion fruit seeds; remove from the heat and let cool.

Pour the glaze on top of the cold cheesecake and refrigerate for at least 30 minutes.

## The mango puree

Meanwhile, peel and pit the mango and cut it into chunks. Put it in a blender or food processor, add the lime juice and sugar, and puree. Refrigerate.

## To serve

Run a sharp knife around the sides of the cheesecake mold to loosen the cake and lift off the mold (or remove the sides of the springform pan). Cut into portions, running the knife under very hot water and wiping it dry after each for a clean cut.

Spread some mango puree on each plate and top with a slice of the cheesecake.

*Brillat-Savarin* **Cheesecake with Mango** and Passion Fruit

# Afterword

I left France when I was twenty, and I didn't look back. I wanted to see the world, and I never thought of returning.

But then France came to me in the person of Marie, who became my wife. Love and the impending birth of our first child brought me back to my homeland. Marie and I have two children now: Tom, born in 2008, and Lily, born in 2011. We also work together: she's the associate managing director of Frenchie to Go, my new venture down the street. She takes care of everything there so I can be in the kitchen and cook!

I lost my family when I was a child, and I found I had to rebuild my life somewhere else before bringing it back home. Because this place is definitely my home: the restaurant, which now has two little sisters, Wine Bar and Frenchie to Go; my wife and kids, with our apartment a block away; and my staff. Our little street, the rue du Nil, is now populated with friends and coworkers, suppliers, and customers. This is the community I've always dreamt of, a community that shares my love of food and the good life.

This book started as a small project, and I didn't realize it would become so meaningful to me. I'm grateful to all my coworkers who were involved, as well as to Djamel, the photographer, who worked in great synergy with us. I am so happy and proud of this English version, which allows me to share my journey and my universe with a whole new community. I hope you too feel my excitement. More than anything, I hope the book will entice you to cook and to explore new flavors.

# Sources

**Amazon**
*www.amazon.com*
Fleur de sel, piment d'Espelette,
Amarena cherries, sweetened chestnut
puree, candied chestnuts, Italian "00"
flour, fine semolina, and trout roe,
among other gourmet products

**Avi Glatt**
*www.aviglatt.com*
Beef cheeks

**Bob's Red Mill**
*www.bobsredmill.com*
French green lentils, fine semolina, and
many other grains

**Camerons**
*www.cameronsproducts.com*
Stovetop smokers and wood chips

**Citarella**
*www.citarella.com*
Grade A foie gras

**D'Artagnan**
*www.dartagnan.com*
Duck magrets and Grade A foie gras
(usually large)

**Modernist Pantry**
*www.modernistpantry.com*
Sheet gelatin

**Murray's**
*www.murrayscheese.com*
A wide range of international cheeses,
including Fourme d'Ambert, Brillat-
Savarin, and burrata

**Penzey's Spices**
*www.penzeys.com*
Vanilla beans and spices of all kinds

**The Spanish Table**
*www.spanishtable.com*
Chorizo, sherry vinegar, and other
Spanish products

........................................................................................................................................

## Selected Wine Merchants

**Kermit Lynch**
*www.kermitlynch.com*

**Rare Wine Company**
*www.rarewineco.com*

**The Wine Hut**
*www.thewinehutnyc.com*

**Wine Searcher**
*www.wine-searcher.com*
An excellent tool for finding local
sources offering many of the wines
in this book

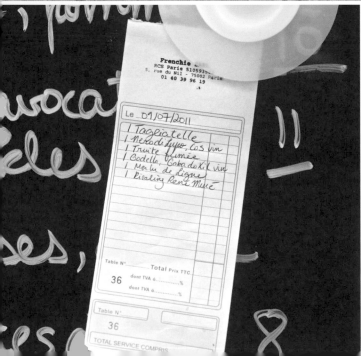

# Acknowledgments

## My deepest thanks to the following people:

Marie, my wife and business associate, for her patience and constant support.

Ann Bramson, for her amazing kindness and wisdom, and the Artisan team; Judith Sutton, for her great recipe testing and editing of the recipes; and Camille Labro, for her translating and rewriting work.

In addition, I owe an enormous amount of gratitude to Djamel Dine Zitout, for his great photographs, as well as for his amazing capacity to adapt to the demands of my job, to listen, and to reassure me in moments of doubt.

Thanks to Alexandre Drouard and Samuel Nahon of Terroirs d'Avenir, for always finding exceptional products, and for enlivening the street with their three shops; to Stéphane Meyer, the forager, for his beautiful wild plants; to Yves-Marie Le Bourdonnec and Sarah and Tim Wilson from Ginger Pig, for their amazing meats; to Pierre André, for his great hams and for his passion; to baker Christophe Vasseur, for his wonderful bread; to Neil's Yard Dairy, for their incredible British cheese; and to all my other suppliers.

Finally, my sincere appreciation goes to the three chefs who inspired me and gave me a chance: Arthur Potts Dawson, Jamie Oliver, and Michael Anthony; and to restaurateurs Nick Jones and Danny Meyer, for sharing their vision of hospitality with me.

# Index